SAINT S
AND RUSSIAN

SAINT SERGIUS AND RUSSIAN SPIRITUALITY

by
PIERRE KOVALEVSKY

Translation by
W. ELIAS JONES

ST. VLADIMIR'S SEMINARY PRESS
Crestwood, NY 10707
1976

First published under the title
SAINT SERGE ET LA SPIRITUALITÉ RUSSE
by Editions du Seuil, Paris [1958]

Library of Congress Cataloging in Publication Data

Kovalevsky, Pierre.
  Saint Sergius and Russian spirituality.

  Translation of Saint Serge et la spiritualité russe.
  Bibliography: p.
  Includes index.
1. Sergii Radonezhskii, Saint, 1314?-1392.
2. Russia—Religious life and customs. I. Title.
BX597.S45K6913   281.9'3 [B]   76-13018
ISBN 0-913836-24-9

ISBN 0-913836-24-9

PRINTED IN THE UNITED STATES OF AMERICA
BY
ATHENS PRINTING COMPANY

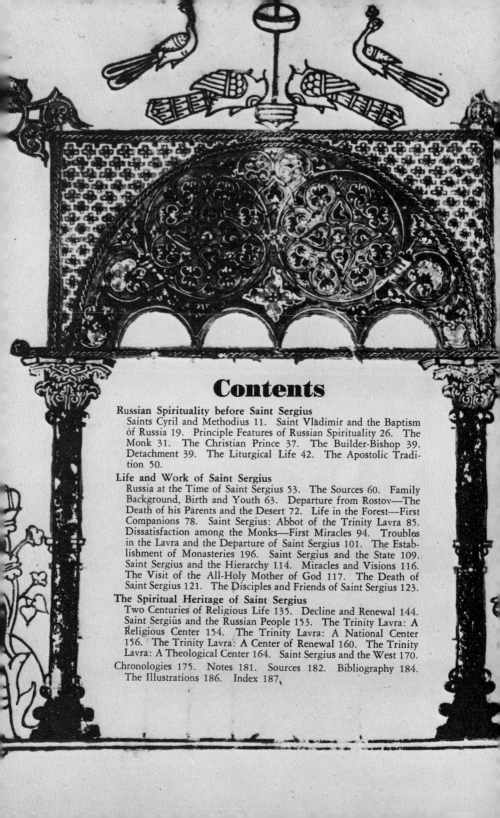

Contents

Nesterov's "Holy Russia" (19th c.).

Among the great spiritual masters, there is one whose influence on the destiny of his country was exceptional. Indeed, one cannot compare him to Moses or to Muhammad, who gave to their nations a new Law. Saint Sergius only applied the Gospel commandments to life; but in doing so he not only served as an example for numerous generations of Christians, but also re-educated his nation. His work is inextricably bound up with the history of Russia from the fourteenth century until our own time.

Saint Sergius drew largely on the treasury of Orthodox spirituality from previous centuries, yet he knew how to adapt this spirituality to the most noble and profound aspirations of his own people. He is not only the greatest saint of Russia, but also a spiritual master whose importance for our times is increasing. His ideal of the monastic life, communal and oriented toward the world, can show the way to many of our contemporaries.

The Russian painter Nesterov, who at the end of the nineteenth century was a restorer of Russian religious painting, has left us a picture which, in reproduction, adorns thousands of Russian homes and which he named "Holy Russia." The picture depicts Christ traveling through the Russian plains and forests, followed by Saint Nicholas, Saint Sergius and Prince Boris, drawing towards Him all the people eager for His words. This picture is completely representative of Russian spirituality, because it is through the country's two patrons, the one adopted and the other its offspring, as well as through the example of the holy Prince Boris, that thousands of souls have been led towards the Savior and have formed that which we call "Holy Russia."

Russian Spirituality Before Saint Sergius

In order to give a complete picture of Orthodox spirituality, it would be necessary to return to the first Christian centuries, to the Doctors of the Eastern Church and to the Desert Fathers. This would be the task of the author of a volume dedicated to Eastern Christian spirituality in general. The present work is especially dedicated to Russian spirituality and to its most universally renowned representative. Russian spirituality, descended from and nourished by the spirituality of the first centuries, clearly dates back only to the time of the Christianization of Russia. We will therefore have to limit ourselves both in time and in space, only returning to the earlier sources inasmuch as they affect Russian spirituality.

Every Christian people passed through a period of initial blossoming which, in most cases, determined its spiritual path. The historical and geographic ambiance played its part in this, but what was decisive for the peoples whose history does not go back to the first Christian centuries was the life of the Church at the moment when they turned towards the faith. The Slavs entered into the family of Christian nations in the

The three great doctors of the Eastern Church: Saint Basil the Great,
Saint Gregory the Theologian (of Nazianzen), Saint John Chrysostom.

9

middle of the ninth and tenth centuries, after the victory of the Church over iconoclasm, at the time of a flowering of the liturgical life. Thus, from the beginning, their spirituality was to be profoundly liturgical, and the icon was to remain at the center of their piety.

What was the situation in the East at the moment when Saints Cyril and Methodius began evangelizing the Slavs? The Byzantine Empire had just overcome the last iconoclastic crisis and the veneration of holy images was solemnly re-established by Empress Theodora and Patriarch Methodius in 843. Henceforth this victory has been commemorated every year on the first Sunday of Lent, which the East calls the "Feast of the Triumph of Orthodoxy." After the Liturgy, there is a special service during which the Church proclaims the true faith (Orthodoxy), commemorates all its defenders and anathematizes those who do not accept the teachings formulated by the seven ecumenical councils.

Towards the middle of the ninth century, the Byzantine Empire entered a brilliant period, under the regency of Empress Theodora and the government of Caesar Bardas. This brilliance was manifested in the arts and sciences, but it is especially the liturgical life, enriched in the preceding century by the works of Saints John of Damascus, Cosmas and Andrew of Crete, that reaches its zenith. The Bulgarians, like the Russians a century later, were won over by the magnificence of the services in Saint Sophia.

Saint John of Damascus was not only the great defender of icons, but also the author of a theology of holy images. He composed the hymns for the services of Sunday and Easter as well as numerous hymns, which later formed the center of the liturgical theology of the Slavic Orthodox peoples. One must not lose sight of the fact that theology properly speaking, which was so flourishing in the Greek Church and in the West, was to perpetuate itself in Russia by the Liturgy, which for a long time, especially in difficult periods, would be the nation's only refuge. Along with Saint John of Damascus we find Saint Cosmas of Maium, who composed the hymns of Holy Week, and Saint Andrew of Crete, author of the Great Canon of Lent.

If the Byzantine Empire was going through a period of internal peace as well as one of literary and artistic activity, its external situation was difficult. New enemies appeared in the north and threatened the capital. They were the Bulgarians, a people of Asiatic ancestry, whose first territory was beyond the Volga but who in the seventh century settled at the mouth of the Danube and who in the eighth century conquered a large part of the Balkans, inhabited by the Slavs. The Bulgarians, who were in due course Slavicized, adopted the Slavic language and the customs of the country. Byzantine politics in the middle of the ninth century tended to draw them into the sphere of imperial influence and to Christianize them. Another threat came from the Norman Vikings, who from the end of the eighth century attacked the Byzantine colonies on the Black Sea. They also fought against the Khazars, who were allied to the Byzantine Empire. Greek engineers had to fortify the Khazar city of Sarkel on the Don against the destructive raids of Vikings (833). It is through the Khazars that Christianity penetrated into Russia, there to take root and spread to Kiev. Further influences coming from the Caucasus also were very strong at the time of the formation of the state of Saint Vladimir.

Thus, in the middle of the ninth century, the Byzantine Empire had two new external problems to resolve: the Christianization of the Balkan Slavs, above all those who occupied the regions under the control of the Bulgars, and then the Christianization of the Eastern Slavs, the Russians, who lived in the vicinity of the Khazar Empire. The religious history of the Slavic peoples and of the Russians in particular began when Byzantium decided to use spiritual forces to draw them into its sphere of influence.

SAINTS CYRIL AND METHODIUS

The great task of evangelizing the Slavic peoples and of initiating them into Christian culture fell upon two brothers, Constantine (Cyril) and Methodius. Saints Cyril and Methodius, sons of the Greek governor of Thessalonica, were born around 827. The entire region around the city in which they spent their childhood was peopled with Slavs, and the two brothers knew to perfection the language spoken in their province. They received a brilliant education in Constantinople, but they soon left the world. For a time Methodius held an important administrative post, but then he withdrew to Mount Olympus. Constantine left the capital for a monastery on the edge of the Black Sea. Brought back to Constantinople against his will, he became a professor at the Patriarchal Academy and a librarian of Saint Sophia. An eminent theologian and a greatly-gifted orator, he took part in the controversy with the iconoclastic ex-Patriarch John VII. In 851, the Arab Caliph asked the Emperor to send him scholars in order that they might discuss the true faith. Constantine went on the embassy and surprised all with his learning. He then joined his brother on Mount Olympus where,

for several years, they prepared themselves for evangelizing the Slavic peoples. Saints Cyril and Methodius, using the Bulgarian dialect of the vicinity of Thessalonica as a base, translated the New Testament and the liturgical books into the Slavic language. This then became Church Slavonic, which to this day is the liturgical language of Orthodox Slavs.

Events would soon hasten and even force the Byzantine Empire to take urgent measures. On June 17 and 18, 860, the Vikings and the Russians attacked Constantinople but were pushed back. After this raid, Patriarch Photius decided to send his best missionary into the Khazar territory, in order to baptize the Slavic elements and to separate them, if possible, from the Vikings. Constantine-Cyril left for Cherson and, as his "Life" relates it, found the relics of Saint Clement of Rome not far from this city. This event was to have an exceptional importance for his mission and for the Russian Church in particular. The feast of the deliverance of Constantinople from the Russo-Viking threat (the Protection of the Holy Virgin), set on October 1, was forgotten by the Greeks but is still celebrated in Russia today. Furthermore, the account of the miraculous discovery of the relics of Saint Clement, who died as a martyr in the Crimea in 101, became one of the foundations of Russian piety as well as one of the pillars of the apostolic tradition in that land.

Saint Cyril's mission to the Khazars (a people from Asia Minor, probably descendants of the Hittites of the Old Testament and later converted to Judaism) had no direct results. However, it is very probable that the Apostle to the Slavs brought numerous Russians living in the Khazar area to the Christian faith. From this time on, we find Christians in Kiev, where they built a church dedicated to the prophet Elias.

Saint Cyril took with him to Constantinople some of the relics of Saint Clement, which he would later give to Pope Hadrian II. An account kept by the chronicles says elsewhere that during his mission to the land of the Khazars he found some Slavic texts, written in bizarre letters, similar to those of the Georgians and Armenians. These letters are known as the glagolithic alphabet. Saint Cyril replaced them with a

Saints Cyril and Methodius with the Emperor Michael (fresco, Kiev, 12th c.).

13

Saints Cyril and Methodius translating the Holy Scriptures into Slavonic (miniature, Radziwill manuscript, 14th c.).

much simpler alphabet, admirably adapted to the Slavic sounds and based on Greek letters. He added the letter "b" and the four sibilants. This is known as the Cyrillic alphabet.

In 862, the two missionary brothers went to evangelize the Bulgars. The prince of the Bulgars, Bogoris (Boris), was baptized, as well as all of his people. In 864, at the invitation of Prince Rastislav, Saints Cyril and Methodius went to Moravia. The translation of the Holy Scriptures and of the liturgical books into Slavonic had a great importance. On the one hand, by the choice of corresponding Slavonic words, it witnessed to the meaning that Greek theologians gave to certain theological terms. On the other hand, its purely missionary influence was considerable. For the term "catholic" (*katholikos*), they chose the Slavonic word *soborny* (conciliar, that which unites all); the Greek term *kharis* (grace) was rendered as *blagodat'* (a gift of that which is good, useful). These translations of Greek theological terms played a very important role in the development of Slavic (and particularly Russian) theology and spirituality, just as the Latin translation of *kharis* as *gratia* had a determining influence on Western theology and spirituality.

The mission of Saints Cyril and Methodius to Moravia-Pannonia established for following centuries the pattern for relations between the Germanic and Slavic peoples and was the starting-point of the struggle between two missionary

14

movements: that of Rome and that of Constantinople. The formation, finally, of a powerful Christian Bulgarian kingdom, located between the two capitals of the old Roman Empire, and its resolve to assert its religious independence was decisive for the Christianization of Russia a century later.

As early as the year 805, Charlemagne, by the Capitulary of Thionville, had established the western border of the Slavic expansion into Central Europe. It went through Hamburg, Magdeburg, Erfurt, Regensburg and went down to the Adriatic Sea. But the "Drang nach Osten" of the Germanic peoples could not stop at this imaginary line. It was the bishops of Salzburg and Regensburg who took the initiative in Latinizing the neighboring Slavic peoples.

Saints Cyril and Methodius succeeded entirely in their mission and Christianized all of Moravia and a part of Pannonia, but as early as 866 their mission clashed with that of the bishops of Regensburg. The Apostles to the Slavs had everywhere introduced services in the vernacular, the Byzantine rite and the Creed without the addition of the *filioque*. The Germanic bishops only allowed Latin, services according to the Roman rite and the Creed with the *filioque*, an addition introduced in their countries by the Germanic emperors but not sanctioned by the Popes. Relations between Rome and Constantinople at this time were normal and even friendly. The recent works of Fr. Dvornik show us that Patriarch Photius was very open to relations with the West, whereas his predecessor, Ignatius, assisted by the Studite monks, had declared himself hostile to any contact with Rome (*The Photian Schism, History and Legend*, Cambridge, 1948).

Thus, it was quite natural for Saints Cyril and Methodius, in 867, to take their dispute with the Germanic bishops before Pope Nicholas I (858-867). They went to Rome, carrying the relics of Saint Clement, and were received with great pomp at the gates of the city by the newly-elected pontiff, Hadrian II (867-872). The Pope placed the New Testament and the liturgical books in Slavonic on the altar of one of the Roman churches and solemnly confirmed the right of the Slavic peoples to celebrate their services in their own language, according to the Byzantine rite and without the addition of the *filioque*. Saint Methodius was consecrated Bishop of Moravia by the Pope and continued his missionary work.

15

Saint Cyril died in Rome and was buried in the Church of Saint Clement.

Despite formal orders from the sovereign pontiff, the Germanic Empire and the bishops of Salzburg and Regensburg continued the fight against Saint Methodius' mission. He was imprisoned and was only released at the end of three years by a formal decree from Pope John VIII (872-882). He made a second trip to Rome and was elevated by the Pope to the dignity of Archbishop of Moravia and Pannonia and papal legate (873). Despite the continually growing opposition of the Germanic missionaries, he was able for twelve years to work on the organization of his archdiocese. He died during a trip to Constantinople in 885.

After the death of Saint Methodius, all of his work was completely destroyed. The Germanic bishops forbade services in Slavonic or in the Byzantine rite and introduced the *filioque* into the Creed. The students of the Apostles to the Slavs were dispersed and went to Bulgaria and to the East into the not-yet-Christianized regions of Poland and Russia.

Two years later, the papacy entered a very difficult period, characterized for Catholic historians by the expression: "The Church in the hands of the laity." For more than a century, the throne of Rome was the stake for several local patrician families, and the authority of the Bishop of Rome was shaken. At about the same time, a new Christian power entered the most brilliant period of its history and played a decisive role in the Christianization of the Russian people. Under King Simeon the Great (893-927), Bulgaria became a European power, heir of the civil and religious culture of Byzantium. The intensity of the religious life corresponded to the growth of the arts and sciences. The heresy of the Cathars (Bogomils), which had come from the East, provoked a lively reaction by ascetics. The best-known representative of the religious movement that opposed the heresy was Saint John of Ryla (d. 946).

Numerous copies of the texts of Holy Scripture and the liturgical books were made and served to Christianize Russia at the end of the century. Likewise, Bulgarian liturgical chants were accepted by the Kievan state. In 927, the archbishops of Ochrid, the capital of Bulgaria, received their religious independence (autocephaly) from the Patriarchs of Constantinople.

In 967, the army of the Russian prince Sviatoslav conquered the entire east of the country, but according to recent research, he spared the churches and the clergy everywhere. After the departure of the Russians, this part of Bulgaria was occupied by Byzantium, but the western part passed through a new period of flowering under King (Tsar) Samuel (983-1014). Even after the kingdom fell in 1018, the Bulgarian Church maintained its independent position and the Archbishop of Ochrid played an active part in the organization of the Russian Church.

What, then, were the Christian sponsors of the Russian people, who were a powerful state on the eve of their conversion? The first Christian infiltrations came through the Caucasus, where there were two very ancient churches: that of Armenia (founded *ca.* 300) and that of Georgia (founded in 325). The influences which came through the Caucasus made themselves felt especially in the realm of art.

Direct Byzantine influence, which went through the Crimea and the Greek colonies of the Black Sea, was rather limited. It only became preponderant towards the middle of the eleventh century. Bulgarian influence, however, was decisive. On the one hand, the Russian occupation opened the way for economic exchanges, which soon became cultural and religious exchanges. On the other hand, it was completely natural for Russian Christians to turn towards a country where they could find holy books and liturgical texts in Slavonic.

Relations with the West were rather difficult. After the dispersion of Saint Methodius' mission, several missionaries arrived in the western provinces of Russia (Volynia, Podolia, perhaps Smolensk). They were persecuted for their attachment to the Byzantine rite and services in Slavonic. They were opposed to any relations with the West, as much from a national perspective as well as a religious one. Other Slavic countries suffered almost the same fate as did Moravia. In Poland, there were two religious metropolitanates: that of Sandomir, with services in Polish and the Byzantine rite, and that of Gniezno, which used the Roman rite and Latin as its liturgical language. It was not until the eleventh century that

17

the Western mission imposed itself on the entire country.

Nevertheless, the first relations of Russia with the Christian West date from the middle of the tenth century. In 959, the Grand Princess Olga, regent of the Kievan state, sent envoys to the Germanic Emperor Otto I. Saint Olga was the first Russian princess to embrace Christianity. Her baptism should be dated around the years 954-955. According to one historical account, she was baptized in Kiev by Bulgarian priests serving at the Church of Saint Elias. According to another account, it was during her visit to Constantinople in 955 that she embraced Christianity, with Emperor Michael and Patriarch Ignatius as her sponsors. The Grand Princess Olga had a great influence over her grandson, Vladimir, but her son Sviatoslav remained pagan until his death. The Russian people have kept a grateful memory of Princess Olga and the Church has honored her with the title "blessed."

The embassy to Emperor Otto I was followed by that of Archbishop Adalbert of Trier to Russia, but this was fruitless. It was the grandson of the Blessed Olga who would have the glory of Christianizing his people. At the time of Saint Olga, any mission coming from the Germanic countries would have been considered as suspect. Furthermore, Olga the Wise (as the people often called her) wanted to initiate her people into the faith in a language that was familiar to them.

Princess Olga speaks with the Byzantine Emperor and receives baptism (miniature, 11th c.).

Saint Vladimir (Moscow kremlin, 16th c.).

SAINT VLADIMIR AND
THE BAPTISM OF RUSSIA

Saint Vladimir was not only the Apostle to Russia but also the founder of a great Christian state which, under his immediate successors, occupied a place of eminence among the European states. Born around the year 940, son of Prince Sviatoslav and a Slavic woman, Vladimir became, in 980, the sovereign of a kingdom which stretched from the Black Sea to the Baltic. A convinced pagan, like most Viking chiefs,

19

he made sacrifices and the worship of idols a state duty. We know the case of a Christian father who refused to give his son to the pagan gods and who died as a martyr with his child in Kiev. However the Grand Prince practiced a wide hospitality. He had inherited from his mother certain traits of a Slavic character. Periods of contrition sometimes followed his fits of violence.

Prince Vladimir subjugated the tribes in the Russian plain who were still independent, made war with the Lithuanians and took away Galicia and Bukhovina from King Mieszko of Poland. But increasingly he turned his attention towards Bulgaria, which under Tsar Samuel was shining in its final brilliance. The Grand Prince could see there the benefits of Christian civilization, and he intended to let his people profit from it. Moreover, he had been prepared. There were three possibilities for him: he could turn to Rome, to Constantinople or to Ochrid. Neither Rome nor Constantinople could give Russia missionaries who spoke the language. Only Bulgaria offered the prince a Slavic clergy and liturgical books in Slavonic and willingly granted to the new state its hierarchical independence.

The decision to convert was made after mature reflection and the conversion was, as we shall see, total. The chronicler reports that Prince Vladimir had sent envoys to different countries—to the Christians, the Muslims and the Jews—in order to question them on their faith. On the return from their voyage, the ambassadors affirmed that the divine office in the Saint Sophia Cathedral of Constantinople had made an unforgettable impression on them: "We thought that we were in heaven and no longer on earth." It is very significant that it was a liturgical recollection which, according to the chronicle, led Prince Vladimir to decide to embrace Christianity according to the Byzantine rite.

The glory of Constantinople at this time was reflected in that of the Holy Mountain (Mount Athos), which since 960 (the date of the foundation of the Lavra by Saint Athanasius) had become an example of Christian life for the newly-converted peoples. One of the founders of Russian monasticism, Saint Anthony of Kiev, spent several years on Mount Athos before going to live in the caves not far from Kiev.

According to recent research, events relating to the baptism of Russia unfolded in the following way: In the course of the summer of 987, the imperial city found itself under the threat of a revolt of the Byzantine legions of Asia Minor, which, with Bardas Phocas at their head, were marching on Constantinople. Bardas proclaimed himself emperor and the two *basileis* (emperors), Constantine and Basil, found themselves obliged to appeal to their neighbors for help. They then asked the Grand Prince to assist them. The Grand Prince of Kiev consented to lend assistance to the emperors, but he asked for the hand of their sister Anne in exchange. They, on their part, required his conversion to Christianity. The Grand Prince accepted, and in the spring of 980 he, along with his people, was baptized by the Bulgarian priests who lived in Kiev.

At the beginning of the summer, he entered the battle at the head of six thousand of his best warriors and inflicted a bloody defeat on Bardas near Scutari (Chrysopolis). The two brother-emperors, relieved of the threat, lagged in fulfilling their promise. Bardas raised new troops and marched on the capital a second time. Grand Prince Vladimir considered himself obliged to continue the campaign and, on April 13, 989, he again defeated Phocas at Abydos. Several days later, Phocas died of an embolism. Constantine and Basil, now that their empire was safe, no longer thought of the marriage of their sister. At the end of his patience, Vladimir, on the way home, laid siege to the richest and most powerful Byzantine colony on the Black Sea, Cherson. The siege lasted several months, and the city fell into Vladimir's hands only after he had caused a detour of the aquaducts. The emperors then decided to send Princess Anne, who arrived in the Crimea with numerous attendants, among whom were several Greek bishops. At the time of the siege, the Grand Prince had received envoys from the Pope bearing a plan for the hierarchical organization of the Russian Church, but the negotiations had no positive result.

Prince Vladimir, accompanied by Princess Anne, returned to Kiev as a victor (990) and set about organizing a Christian state. He brought with him from the Crimea not only the famous bronze symbol of imperial power, but also the relics of Saint Clement of Rome, which he placed in the newly-built Cathedral of the Dormition. The Greek bishops

21

did not follow him to Kiev but returned to Constantinople. The Grand Prince was assisted in his effort to evangelize the country by Archbishop Michael, who was probably of Balkan origin, and by Bishop Joachim, a native of the region of Cherson.

The failure of the negotiations with Rome and Byzantium over the problem of hierarchical organization in no way affected the friendly relations between Kiev and the two capitals of Christendom. Until recently a letter was preserved, dated in 1007, from Prince Vladimir to the Germanic Emperor Otto II. As for the Papal envoy, the Camaldolese Bruno-Boniface, who had come to evangelize the Asiatic people known as the Pechenegs, he received a warm welcome in Kiev. At the end of the Grand Prince Vladimir's reign, numerous foreign colonies had settled in Kiev and built their chapels. The Russian capital, as early as this period, had become a point of contact between peoples of East and West.

Christianity quickly imbued the life and psychology of the people. The prince set the example. Never was a conversion more complete or richer in consequences. The contemporaries of Saint Vladimir are unanimous in affirming that the character and the life-style of the prince had undergone a radical transformation. He appeared gentle and humane, whereas formerly he had been cruel and violent.

Under his impetus, the empire of Kiev was, from the end of the tenth century, the scene of a unique social experiment, which did appear until much later in Europe. All of the poor and aged became the object of organized social assistance. Provisions and items of great necessity were delivered to them. Porters traveled through the streets of Kiev with the mission of seeking out the sick and infirm who were unable to present themselves at the palace in order there to receive their aid, which came from the cash-box of the prince. This old-age security was not a specialty of the city of Kiev alone, but an institution of the whole Kievan state. The Grand Prince consulted with the bishops on affairs of state, reorganized the courts and abolished the death penalty. His hospitality was legendary, his personal life was marked with the greatest piety. With his last wife, Anne of Byzantium, and

Princess Anne of Kiev (Kiev, 11th c.).

his two younger sons, Boris and Gleb, he formed a profoundly Christian family.

The influence of Saint Vladimir extended for several generations. His granddaughter Anne, the wife of King Henry I
of France, continued the tradition of her grandfather at Senlis. After the death of the King (August 4, 1060), she became the regent of the Kingdom of France. Anne established
her residence at Senlis, where she founded the convent of Saint
Vincent and began the distribution of provisions to the poor

23

Great Prince Yaroslav (Novgorod, 12th c.).

of the city. This custom remained until the French Revolution. Pope Nicholas II addressed to the Queen a letter in which he exalted her Christian social action.

It was under Vladimir's son, Yaroslav the Wise, that the Kievan state reached its zenith. The importance of Kiev in the eleventh century has been summarized as follows: "The prosperity of the state of Yaroslav (1019-1054) developed

The Cathedral of Saint Sophia in Kiev (11th c.) according to a modern reconstruction.

marvellously. His capital, which grew from day to day, became the emporium of an intense commerce which linked Germany and Scandinavia to the Byzantine Empire, the West to the East. It was so prosperous that in the area of monumental art, it became, after Constantinople, the capital of the European world. Rome at the time was no more than a mere phantom: Abandoned by the emperors, devastated by the barbarians, continuously torn apart by local factions, it was nothing more than ruin and misery." (Maurice Paléologue, "Anna Iaroslavna, Reine de France.")

During the reign of Yaroslav, the arts were freed from a slavish imitation of Byzantium. The most beautiful monument of this period, the Cathedral of Saint Sophia in Kiev (1025), shows traces of influences from different countries. The masonry facings, for example, are of Mesopotamian origin. Schools opened in Kiev and the first chronicles were composed. The monasteries were sources of civilization. Especially important was the Lavra of the Caves. There bishops and missionaries were prepared to evangelize the north of the country. It was also this monastery which spread the art of icons and of frescoes.

This brilliant period, which ended so tragically in 1240 with the destruction of Kiev during the Mongol invasion, saw the crystalization of Russian spirituality. Kievan Russia progressively transmitted its spiritual treasury during the twelfth century and the beginning of the thirteenth century to the newly-created principalities of the north and to Novgorod, which was the only cultural center which remained intact at the time of the Mongol occupation. After the destruction of Kievan Russia, the populace was obliged to flee towards the forests of the north. The south of the country was completely devastated. Russian spirituality then entered a new period. Having passed through terrible tests, it was renewed and transformed by Saint Sergius. The first two hundred and fifty years of Christian life in Russia (990-1240) form a whole in terms of spirituality. It is necessary to grasp the most striking traits of this period in order in turn to understand the Russian spirituality of the post-Mongol period.

PRINCIPLE FEATURES OF RUSSIAN SPIRITUALITY

Drawing on a treasury amassed through the centuries by the Church, the Russian people from the beginning impressed on it certain national features. All too often have people tried to explain the peculiarities of Russian spirituality by means of the geographical conditions in which the Russians developed at the beginning of their history. A Catholic theologian of Russian origin has insisted very specifically on the influence "of the immense and monotonous plains, of the limitless horizons which forged the Russian soul." He adds that "the consciousness of the well-defined form, of which the Latins and the Greeks are so proud, is foreign to them." According to him the characteristic features of the Russian people are freedom of spirit, a love for pilgrimages, a detachment from the goods of this world and a revolt against the bourgeois world. (Kologrivof, *Essai sur la Sainteté en Russie*, Paris: Beyaert, 1953.)

The latter affirmations are relatively accurate, but it is necessary to be extremely prudent if one wishes to justify them by geographical considerations. Russian spirituality de-

The Volga.

veloped at a time when the steppes of southern Russia were
the "wild field" whence came all of the country's enemies.
Kievan Russia struggled continuously against these areas of
infinite horizons. Popular Russian literature from the pre-
Mongol period was full of the gestes of heroes who defended
the state against the steppe. Furthermore, Russia was his-
torically a country of rivers. All of the cultural centers were
established along the long rivers, not in the plains. After the
Mongol invasion, the southern populace fled to the west and
to the north, and the cultural and spiritual center moved to
the forest region. The vast southern expanses did not become

27

Russian *Princes Boris and Gleb (icon, 14th c.).*

Russian until the end of the eighteenth century. Finally, one must not exaggerate the freedom of spirit of the Russian people. Certainly it exists, but it is constantly limited by their sense of community.

We believe that there is another explanation for this freedom of spirit, this detachment from material goods, this love of pilgrimages: this explanation arises out of the Gospel. The Russian people accepted the Gospel message and applied it to their lives with an extreme radicalism. Russia has always been attracted to extremes, whether towards the good or towards the evil. But there was also always the consciousness of being a sinner: thus this intense movement towards holiness, this desire for purification and transfiguration which not only humanity, but every creature must attain. This is also the source of Russia's ardent and idealistic desire for universal salvation, its universalism. The name "Holy Russia" is not an empty title, because for the Russian people the ideal of holiness represents the highest value. The ideal towards which it tends is not one of well-being, but one of holiness: such is the basis of Russian spirituality.

The commandments of Christ must be carried out and His life must be taken as an example. The people called the monks "like unto Christ." We have seen how the Gospel precepts were taken seriously by the Grand Prince Vladimir. His two youngest sons went even to martyrdom in order "innocently to suffer the Passion." Among the virtues of these princes, who were defenders of the faith, the people especially glorified their "suffering." He who had set an example of the Christian life but had not suffered for his brothers was not canonized. "Innocent suffering" was one of the most characteristic traits of the Russian saint. The first Russians whose holiness was proclaimed by the people, despite certain hesitations by the clergy, were those who suffered the Passion after the example of the Savior.[1]

The Grand Prince Vladimir died on July 15, 1015, and was succeeded by his adopted son, Sviatopolk. The people would have preferred the two young princes, Boris and Gleb, born of Princess Anne of Byzantium and whose virtues they knew. The princes would not consent to raising a hand

28

against their older brother: "May he be as a father to us,"
they said to their troops, who were inciting them to march on
Kiev. Nevertheless, fearing that he would be dethroned by
the people, Sviatopolk sent emissaries to assassinate his two
brothers. Instead of resisting, they disbanded their army and
prepared for death. Prince Boris was attending Matins and

reading the Psalms when his brother's emissaries arrived. He stood, as his "Life" states, before the icon of the Savior and prayed: "Lord, Thou didst suffer for our sins; make me worthy to suffer for Thee. I do not die at the hand of my enemies, but at the hand of my brother. Do not hold him responsible for this assassination as a sin." Then he received Communion and lay down peacefully. The assassins ran him through with their spears. One of the servants who wished to cover his body was also killed. When Prince Gleb learned of the death of his brother, he said: "You have received grace from God. Beseech Him that I also may suffer as you did. I would much rather be with you than remain in this world which is full of evil." The prince was found by the assassins in a boat in the middle of the river. His body was abandoned in a forest.

The Russian people gave Prince Sviatopolk the surname "like Cain" and proclaimed Princes Boris and Gleb as saints. Their canonization, the first in Russia (1020), five years after their death, was almost imposed by the people. Despite miracles at their tomb and the incorruptibility of their bodies, the hierarchy was reserved, being unable to proclaim them as martyrs for the faith. Popular piety designated them by the name of "saints-who-innocently-suffered-the-Passion" or "Passion-bearers." Archbishop John of Ochrid consented to preside at their canonization, but a half-century later, the Greek metropolitan of Kiev protested against this creation of a new category of saints by the Russians.

It is significant that the glory of Saints Boris and Gleb was explained in their "Life" by the following fact: "They took upon themselves our sins, committed inasmuch as we were still pagans." The "Life" of Saints Boris and Gleb remained the favorite reading of the Russian people, and their tomb in Vyshgorod was a place of national pilgrimage.

The number of saints who were "Passion-bearers" is limited to three. Besides Princes Boris and Gleb, the people venerated Prince Igor of Chernigov, whose life was exemplary. He left power in order not to be the cause of a dynastic conflict, but he was nevertheless assassinated in the monastery to which he had retired. The prince was praying before an icon of the Holy Virgin when he was killed. His canonization occured three years later (1150).

The monastic life.

THE MONK

The ideal of the monastic life developed as early as the eleventh century, but it did not take its definitive form until the time of Saint Sergius. Its principle was that of the ceno-bitic life, oriented towards the world. The monk was poor, his life ascetical, but full of active charity. The monastic community tended not only towards personal perfection, but also towards the sanctification of the life of the people. Thus the monastery was a living center, whose educating influ-ence extended to the entire surrounding population. The lev-eling effect of the Rule was compensated by an absolute obedience to the Abbot, who had to be not only an example of life for the monks, but also an educator who applied the

Rule according to the measure of each. Asceticism, often very severe, nevertheless excluded any exaltation. Even the "fools-for-Christ," which some wrongly consider as a specifically Russian category of asceticism, were exempt from the excesses of their Western peers.

A Gospel text was always present in the spirit of a believing Russia: "But seek first His kingdom and His righteousness, and all these things shall be yours as well" (Matthew 6:33).

The account of the Last Judgment remained alive in the spirit of Russia. It never forgot that those who had fed and given drink, who had welcomed strangers and visited the sick and the prisoners, would inherit the kingdom of heaven (Matthew 25:31-46). Thus one of the two great Russian theologians of this period, Saint Abraham of Smolensk, put up a tableau representing the Last Judgment at the entrance to the church of his monastery.

It is true that the beginnings of Russian monasticism knew the attempt to direct the life of the monk towards an Athonite ideal: eremitical, completely separated from this world. But this attempt failed, despite the deep spirituality and exemplary ascetic life of its initiator, Saint Anthony (983-1073). A native of the city of Liubech in the province of Chernigov, he left his home at a very early age and went to Mount Athos. There he lived the life of an anchorite and was one of the first amongst the numerous Russians who came throughout the centuries to populate the Holy Mountain. The two types of monastic life, eremitic and cenobitic, were flourishing at this time on Mount Athos, but there was no Russian monastery. Therefore, Saint Anthony became a monk in a Greek monastery.

He returned to Russia in 1013, but the political events and the fratricidal war which occurred after the death of Saint Vladimir obliged him to return to the Holy Mountain. It was not until 1028 that, on the formal order of his spiritual father, the monk Theoktistos, he returned to Kiev to found the first Russian monastery there. He found several monks who had dug out caves in the cliffs of the Dnieper. Saint Anthony occupied that of the priest Hilary (Hilarion), fu-

Saint Anthony and the foundation of the Monastery of the Caves in Kiev.

33

ture Metropolitan of Kiev, who had been called to serve the princely chapel at Berestov. The glory of Saint Anthony was so great that it attracted to him numerous monks who wanted to live under his direction. But since the founder refused to become a superior each one lived in his own cave, and thus they formed only a grouping of hermits. Their life was very hard and full of renunciation.

One day, a rich lord named Barlaam arrived, bringing numerous gifts to the monastery. He placed his princely robes at Saint Anthony's feet and asked to be received into the number of monks. He soon became the first abbot and directed the little community until 1057. Saint Anthony died in 1073, venerated by all. A counsellor whose word was heeded, he remained apart from the life of his abbey. His grave remained hidden, and his canonization did not occur until much later.

Nevertheless, the ideal of the monk completely detached from the interests of this world remained alive. Throughout the centuries, hundreds of Russians went to Mount Athos, where the Monastery of Saint Panteleimon had been founded. The monastery exists to this day, though only a handful of monks remain.

Saint Theodosius, who arrived at the Monastery of the Caves in 1032, took charge of it after the departure of Abbot Barlaam. It was Theodosius who incarnated the ideal of the monk in the eyes of the Russian people. Born in 1008 near Kiev, as a child he moved with his parents to Kursk. (In the nineteenth century, this city was the home of the greatest Russian saint of recent times, Saint Seraphim.) Theodosius loved the divine offices; he sang, read and prepared the eucharistic breads for the church. His mother considered his occupations unworthy of a young man who belonged to a rich family and reproached him for his ascetical life. At the age of twenty-four he left his maternal home and became a monk at the Monastery of the Caves in Kiev. His mother found him four years later and, at his suggestion, took the habit of a nun.

Theodosius began by installing a church which could hold the hundred monks gathered around him; this could not be done in the underground chapel. He then built living quarters which replaced the caves and introduced the Studite

Kiev's Monastery of the Caves today.

Rule into the abbey. This remained the general rule for most Russian monasteries. An abridged text had been brought to Kiev by Metropolitan George, but Saint Theodosius wanted a more complete text. He sent a monk to Constantinople who brought him the complete text. The Studite Rule deals with the life of the monk and the services celebrated in the abbey. It was composed after the death of Theodore the Studite by his pupils on the basis of his spiritual testament. Saint Theodosius introduced many changes. He instituted four categories of monks: the aspirants, who still wore secular clothing; the associates, without vows, who were dressed as monks; those who had pronounced the little vows; and those who had pronounced the great vows.

The principal rule was absolute obedience to the abbot.

35

Nothing was to be done without his blessing. Saint Theodosius threw into the fire everything that the monks did without his blessing, even food. We shall see how Saint Sergius modified this rule. The monks received daily oral instruction from the abbot. They could not have in their cells private possessions. The abbot visited the cells and closely oversaw the education of each monk. He did it according to the strengths of each and without violence, setting for all an example of a simple and ascetical life.

Poorly clothed, always at work, he chopped wood and carried water like a simple monk during the day and spent the entire evening in prayer. He always appeared joyous and full of charity. He did not restrict his work to the walls of the monastery. He visited the sick and the poor and distributed to them all the gifts which the abbey received. He built a home for the needy of the city. His entire life was oriented towards the world. Every Sunday, a cart left from the monastery, filled with bread for distribution to prisoners.

The abbey was poor, but help always came in time. The holy abbot was not only able to feed his monks but also all those who came to see him and ask his advice. He never feared intervening in the affairs of the principalities when justice was at stake; he defended the weak against the courts.

His abbey soon became a source of bishops and missionaries who went to evangelize the most distant regions. The first national chronicles were composed at the Lavra of the Caves in Kiev; it was there that copies were made of liturgical books and of the Holy Scriptures and that the sciences and the arts were taught. The monastery was the center of the art of Russian icons, which has as its patron Saint Alypius, a monk of Kiev. The art of the fresco was introduced by Byzantine monks who helped in the construction of the Cathedral of the Dormition (1073). (It was destroyed in 1943, during the Second World War.) The Lavra of Kiev produced a number of very important canonized saints. Its importance for Kievan Russia was truly exceptional.[2]

Saint Theodosius died in 1074, and in 1097 his body was found intact. He was canonized in 1108, at the time of the centenary of his birth. He has remained one of the most popular saints in Russia. His "Life," written by the monk Nestor the Chronicler, was reproduced in hundreds of copies

and translated into Serbian and Bulgarian. The organizer of
the Lavra of Kiev has remained for the Russian people the
ideal monk who was able to unite an austere and blameless
life to the work of educating his contemporaries.

*The crown of
Monomachos.*

THE CHRISTIAN PRINCE

The ideal of the Christian prince was personified by
Vladimir Monomachos (1053-1125), a defender of order and
justice. He was a peacemaker who by his moral authority
arbitrated conflicts between the princes. Severe in his application of the law, he only struck the guilty. In his *Admoni-
tion* he describes the life of a Christian prince—a life which,
like that of Saint Vladimir, ought to be motivated by mercy
and industry. He exalted nature, the creation of God, which
should incite us to good works. All of the powers of the
prince should be consecrated to the well-being of his people.
He should never let a supplicant leave without helping him.
Vladimir Monomachos visited the sick and the poor. He
remained in the memory of the people as an example of
Christian virtues, but he was not canonized. Kievan Russia
drew a line between holiness and virtue. Princes were considered saints only if they had suffered.

Another prince, Vsevolod of Novgorod, grandson of Vladimir Monomachos, was also of an exceptional moral greatness. He reformed social life, humanized justice, worked for raising the level of his people, but was nevertheless banished by the citizens of Novgorod. Received by the neighboring city of Pskov, he continued his charitable work there, built the cathedral of the Holy Trinity and died (1138) surrounded by the veneration of the populace. He was canonized as one who had suffered for justice. The third prince, Dovmont, exiled from his estates by the pagan Lithuanians, also settled in Pskov, where he defended the city against the Germans, built churches and set an example of a pious life, devoted to the public well-being. He was also recognized as a saint.

Among the princes who suffered for their country, the place of honor belongs to Alexander Nevsky ("of the Neva") who remained for the people the model defender of the faith and of justice. He was prince of Novgorod at the time of the Mongol invasion. He was exiled by his fellow-citizens and became Grand Prince of all Russia at the most critical moment in Russian history. Exceptionally handsome and possessing an immense greatness of spirit, Prince Alexander (1219-1263) was a legendary hero for many Russians. The Grand Master of the Livonian Order said of him: "I have travelled throughout many countries, I know men and kings, but Alexander of Novgorod compelled my admiration." The Grand Prince Alexander vanquished the Swedes on the Neva in 1240 (thus his surname, Nevsky) and the Teutonic Knights on the ice of the lake in Pskov in 1242. He took upon himself the burden of the difficult negotiations with the Mongols. He had to go to Asia to defend his people, and upon returning from one of these sad missions, he died of exhaustion (1263).

Saint Alexander can be compared to his contemporary, Saint Louis, King of France. Both received a brilliant and excellent education in the same virtues: wisdom, prudence, humility and piety. Both fought against the enemies of the Fatherland and of the Church. Penetrated by a sense of duty to the point of self-renunciation, they were both canonized.

THE BUILDER-BISHOP

Finally, Russian piety honored the great bishops: builders of cathedrals, missionaries to the northern regions and peace-makers for the country. Among those of this first period, Saint Leontius of Rostov, Saint Nikita of Novgorod and Saint Cyril of Turov must be mentioned. The latter, along with Saint Abraham of Smolensk, was a theologian of great merit and the author of ascetical works.

Abraham of Smolensk was not only an eschatological thinker but also the first of the Russian "startsy" ("elders"), monks who received visitors in their cells and guided them in their lives, strengthening their souls. Though he was per-secuted for his theological ideas and his practices as a guide of souls, he overcame all difficulties and remained one of the holy protectors of his city.

DETACHMENT

Lay spirituality is inextricably bound up with the char-acter of the Russian people who, having accepted the Gospel message, kept it faithfully. The most striking characteristic of this spirituality is detachment from the goods of this earth. The feeling for property was not absent from the Russian soul, but they freely said: "Everything belongs to God. God has given, God has taken. It is His holy will." This absence of attachment to the goods of the earth is not unrelated to the constant desire to go to great lengths to seek justice and truth. Nor is it unrelated to the example of going on pil-grimages to the holy places.

From the first centuries of their Christian life, the Rus-sian people were in continual movement. They went to Mount Athos, to the Holy Land, to Bari to venerate Saint Nicholas. Abbot Daniel, who visited Jerusalem in 1106-1108, left us a moving account of one of these pilgrimages. Princes Euphrosyne of Polotsk died in the Holy Land (1173). But there were countless pilgrims who did not leave their country. They went to Kiev and to Vyshgorod to ven-erate the graves of Saint Theodosius and of the princes Boris and Gleb; or very simply, they walked on the highway, seek-

Along the highways, the pilgrims say their prayers.

ing the holy city where justice reigned. The legend of the invisible city of Kitezh, which disappeared under the waters of Clear Lake (Svetloiar), is characteristic of this spiritual state. The famous Russian historian Kliuchevsky, in analyzing the classes of the Russian populace at this time, points out one group that was perpetually in motion and that lived on the name of Christ. These pilgrims spread the lives of the saints, the favorite reading of the Russian people. The blind singers who travelled throughout Russia propagated from one end of the immense country to the other accounts, often embellished with legendary details, of Saint George, Saint Alexis and especially of the "pilgrimages of the Virgin through hell." It is interesting to note that this latter account changed with the times. One added or subtracted new categories of sinners from the list of those who suffered in hell, in accordance with the historical circumstances.

Eschatological problems always haunted the Russian spirit. Here we can but mention the hymn of the *Book of the Dove,* the apocalyptic vision of the heavenly Jerusalem in the life of Saint Andrew, the same vision in the life of Basil the Younger, and the tale of the three pilgrims in the life of Macarius the Roman.

Along with the lives of the saints, the Russian people were nourished with extracts from the Fathers of the Church, such as Saint Ephraim the Syrian, Saint John Climacus, Saint John of Damascus, Saint Nilus of Sinai, but especially Saint John Chrysostom. The anthologies of the works of this latter saint, who was called "Ray of Gold," or "Golden-Mouthed," "Emerald" or "Pearl," circulated throughout Russia in hundreds of copies.

Saint John Chrysostom (Kiev, 12th c.).

We find this influence of Saint John Chrysostom in the "startsy," those guides of souls, those men who struggled against "athumia": the discouragement, the sadness which consumes the soul. Saint John was also loved because he suffered much during his lifetime and taught us that suffering carries with it a lesson both for oneself and for others.

The "fools-for-Christ" appeared in Russia a little later. The three best-known, Saint Procopius of Ustiug, Isidore and John of Rostov, were, moreover, of Western origin, probably Germanic.

THE LITURGICAL LIFE

From the beginning, Russian spirituality flowered in the liturgical life. We have spoken of the impression which the services at Saint Sophia of Constantinople produced on the envoys of the Grand Prince Vladimir. The Russian people were held captive by the beauty of Byzantine Orthodox ceremonies, by their feeling of community, by their symbolism, by the icons and the chants. As Fr. Louis Bouyer says: "The New Rome was able to create a metaphysical thought, a dramatic and lyric poetry, a wisdom of life, the whole achieving an organic unity. The Byzantine liturgy is the heart of this civilization." (*Dieu Vivant*, vol. 21.)

In the Liturgy the Russian people found their ideal of the unity of the temporal and the infinite, of all that is beautiful on this earth, because it was created by God, with all that of which we can only catch a glimpse through the elect, the saints, who surround us. In the holy images, they saw the presence on earth of the Church Triumphant. For them, the Liturgy was a Biblical education as well as a dogmatic one. It brought to life all of the events of the Old and New Testaments and taught theology. The liturgical year, which until the Revolution ruled the entire life of the Russian people, was also the very life of the Church.

Russia was heir to a high theological tradition which had explained in chants and hymns all the great dogmatic truths. For example, the eight "dogmatics" of Saint John of Damascus, sung during Saturday evening Vespers on a revolving basis, constituted thorough theological lessons on the Incar-

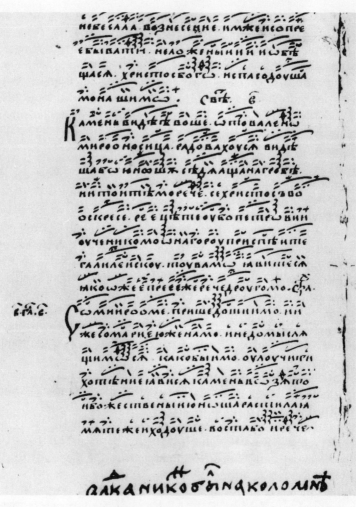

A liturgical manuscript (16th c.).

nation. The Liturgy was an auditory education for the Russians, an "auditory Bible," in much the same way as the Bible in stone of the Gothic cathedrals taught the Western congregations. As books (manuscripts) were rare and most believers could neither read nor write, the system of canonarchs was introduced. The reader, who was supposed to have a beautiful voice and perfect diction, announced a phrase of the chant or Psalm, and the choir or the congregation sang it in the announced "tone."

The twelve great feasts of the Christian calender were celebrated with great fervor, but it was Easter, the feast of feasts, which was the undisputed center of all the liturgical spirituality of the Russian people. Only the Russian language gave Sunday the name of "Resurrection" (voskreseniye), whereas, in Church Slavonic, Sunday was called simply "the day of rest" (nedelya). Easter is celebrated as in no other country. The midnight Matins, followed by a (nocturnal) Liturgy, gathers all the faithful in joy. The doors of the sanctuary remain open throughout the whole week. According to popular belief, all those who die at Easter go directly to Paradise. Even the burial service during the Paschal Week is joyous. The joy is expressed by the custom of kissing three times when Russian Orthodox meet each other throughout the entire Paschal period until the Ascension. It is at Easter that the spirit of fraternal community is most clearly expressed. As for the other feasts, they are not only celebrated as commemorations, but as events which are always new and present. This interior expectation is particularly clear during Holy Week, when all listen, with lighted candles in their hands, to the twelve Passion Gospels or bow before the tomb of our Lord.

The sense of community in the liturgical life is expressed by chanting together, by the litanies intoned by the deacon, which unite the petitions of all the faithful, but especially by the old custom of altar breads, which is particularly carefully preserved in Russia. The worshiper buys an altar bread (prosphora) and sends it to the altar with the names of those who are close to him, both living and dead. The priest removes pieces from the bread, which are placed on the paten with the Lamb (the host). At the end of the Liturgy, he puts them in the chalice, saying the following words: "Wash away, O Lord, the sins of all those remembered here, by Thy precious blood; through the prayers of Thy saints."

The Russian Orthodox is aware of a constant communion with the Church Triumphant, but he guards against any familiarity. He has a great respect for the sacred; for example, a layman cannot touch the altar table. He avoids calling the Holy Virgin directly by her name. All liturgical worship, even when it concerns the Mother of God or the saints, is

The Vladimir icon of the Mother of God (11th c.).

44

Christocentric. The faithful call the Holy Virgin "she who gave birth to God" (Theotokos). For them, she is the Heavenly Mother of all men since our salvation became possible through her act of obedience to the will of God at the time of the Annunciation. All of the old icons of the Virgin portray her with Christ. She was truly the one who kept the words of her divine Son and who passed them on to the apostle of love, Saint John, who is particularly venerated in the East.

The three successive cathedrals of Russia, those of Kiev, Vladimir and Moscow, were dedicated to the Dormition (Assumption) of the Virgin. Two buildings which showed the architectural genius of the Russian people with the greatest power were dedicated to "the Protection of the Mother of God": the cathedral, also named for Saint Basil the Blessed, on Moscow's Red Square (1556), and the church

The church on the Nerl River dedicated to the Protection of the Theotokos (12th c.).

46

on the Nerl (1155). Here is yet another characteristic trait of the veneration of the Holy Virgin: Despite the large number of feasts and icons dedicated to her, the name Mary is rarely given in honor of the Holy Virgin. The countless Marys in Russia usually have Saint Mary Magdalene or Saint Mary of Egypt as their patrons.

Along with the veneration of the Holy Virgin, Russia from the earliest days venerated the Holy Cross, the symbol of Christ's victory over death. The Western crucifix, with a suffering Christ, is unknown in the East. Instead, the Savior is depicted dead on the Cross with peaceful features. In Russia, the Resurrection was often depicted on the reverse side of processional crosses. To the traditional cross with four or six branches, the Russians added a slanting bar which calls to mind the account of the Last Judgment. Those who are on the right of the Savior will go to Heaven and those who are on His left will go down to Hell.

A very special place is reserved in Russia for the veneration of Saint Nicholas, who became the adopted patron of the country. His service is celebrated every Thursday along

47

with that of the apostles. Countless churches are dedicated to him. He is not only venerated by the Christians but also by the pagan population of Siberia. His tomb at Bari, Italy, is the goal of many pilgrimages.

Let us also mention the veneration of the angels. All of the heavenly powers have their feast in November 8. The Russian Christian believes that his guardian angel is the saint whose name he bears. Hence the popular conviction that it is absolutely impossible to have several names at the same time, since each Christian should have only one heavenly protector. The name's day, which is celebrated annually, is called in Russian the "Day of the Angel."

It is in the veneration of the holy icons that the liturgical spirituality of the Russian people finds its deepest expression. "All theology and all dogma can be found there," says Fr. Ildefonse Dierks. (*Les Saintes Icônes,* Chevetogne.) "Icons are the surest and most complete instruction for the people, equal and complementary in this respect to the Divine Liturgy." The icon is the vision of the transfigured world. It shows what man will be after his resurrection. Leonid Ouspensky, a contemporary iconographer, says: "Profane art portrays the reality of the perceptible and emotional world as the artist subjectively sees it. The icon portrays the reality of the Kingdom which is not of this world." (*L'icône, Vision du Monde Spirituel,* Paris: Setor, 1948.) Icons signify the presence in the Church of the Incarnate Son, the Holy Virgin and all the witnesses to the Gospel. Thus, the believer feels surrounded by those who give him the example of holiness. The icon must be blessed and painted with piety. The old iconographers prepared for their task by prayer and fasting. The corner where the family icons are kept is considered as holy and the whole family comes together there for prayer.

Finally, the liturgical spirituality of the Russian people blossomed in the liturgical chants of the Church. The Russian people cultivated polyphonic chant at all times, but the monasteries kept the old, simple and austere monophonic chants.

Byzantine religious architecture underwent a strong development in Russia. Russian churches, decorated with numerous onion domes, which represent lighted candles burning

Cathedral of the Protection of the Theotokos (Saint Basil's) in Moscow.

before the invisible image of God, soar up towards heaven. They are lighter and smaller than in the West. Rather than constructing a few large cathedrals, something which in any case was impossible in a country where there was no stone, the Russians built many smaller churches, often clustered together, again creating a sense both of community and of intimacy.

49

THE APOSTOLIC TRADITION

The last characteristic of the Russian spirituality of this period is the attachment of the Russian people to the apostolic tradition and that of the Church Fathers. The Clementine tradition was still living at that time. It linked the young Russian Church to the Apostles to the Slavs, Saints Cyril and Methodius, who had found the relics of Saint Clement, Bishop of Rome, in Cherson, and at the same time linked them to the Old Rome, as a visible sign of the unity of the Christian world. The relics of Saint Clement of Rome, brought to Kiev by Saint Vladimir in 990, became the symbol of unity with the universal Church. All important acts were carried out before them, and in 1147 their presence justified the consecration of Metropolitan Clement without the blessing of the Patriarch of Constantinople.

The legend of Saint Andrew the Apostle's mission and voyage to Russia developed along with the definitive establishment of the Greek hierarchy in Kiev. It was through this legend that the patron of Byzantium became one of the patrons of Russia. This legend later became one of the pillars of the apostolic tradition in Russia. The Clementine tradition disappeared with the loss of the saint's relics, which perished in a fire at the time of the Mongol invasion of Kiev in 1240.

Constantinople accorded to the Russian Church a place that was not equal to its importance. It was ranked as the sixty-seventh diocese of the Patriarchate. Despite this inequity, the Russian Church did not request autonomy until the Council of Florence, becoming independent from Constantinople only when the Mother Church signed the formula of union with Rome.

This desire for unity and communion with all the parts of the Church constitutes a striking feature of this early period. In 1051, when political difficulties between Kiev and Constantinople obliged the Russians to elect their metropolitan without consulting the Patriarch, they stressed in the act of election the existence of communion with the other patriarchates. In 1054, after the schism between East and West, Papal legates returned to Rome through Kiev, where they were received with all the honors befitting their rank. In 1087, when the citizens of Bari, Italy, obtained the relics of Saint Nicholas from the East, the Russian Church instituted a feast which it still keeps on May 9. In 1106, Anthony the Roman arrived at Novgorod. He became abbot of one of the famous Russian monasteries and was canonized.

The first period, which stretches from the conversion of Russia in 988 to the Mongol invasion in 1240, was decisive in the formation of Russian spirituality. The Mongol yoke made the Russian people pass through a terrible material and moral test. The old Kievan culture was almost completely destroyed. A new culture began to develop, but it required enormous sacrifice. At the most critical moment, when all of the people's energies were directed towards unity and the liberation of the land, when their spiritual and moral energies were still dispersed, the great teacher of the Russian people arose to set right their spirits and lead them in the true way. This guide was Saint Sergius.

The Life and Work of Saint Sergius

It is impossible to understand the life of Saint Sergius and the importance of his work without having a precise idea of the changes which took place after the fall of Kiev, the old capital of Russia, and the transfer of the national center to the north-east. Two facts dominated Russian life at the beginning of the fourteenth century, the time of Saint Sergius' birth: the division of the country into a large number of independent principalities, and the Mongol yoke which had weighed heavily on the country for the last seventy-five years.

The divisions originated in the system introduced into Kievan Russia by Grand Prince Yaroslav the Wise in 1054. In accordance with the law of succession, the country was divided into as many principalities as there were male heirs. The principality of Kiev, which carried with it the title of Grand Prince, went to the oldest male and not to the direct heir. Not only did this system lead to the continual parcelling out of the country, but also to wars of fratricide and struggles for control of the principality of Kiev. In the middle of the thirteenth century, this divided country could not withstand the Mongol invaders; the principalities were conquered and devastated one after the other. Ancient Russia had possessed a regime of popular assemblies (*veche*) and a ruling class

The Tartar invasions.

which played an important role in the life of the state. In
certain principalities, the role of the assembly was preponderant. For example, in the state of Novgorod, the prince
was only the head of the army and could be dismissed by the
assembly. According to the ancient formula, they would
"show him the way out." A reaction against this parcelling-
out and against the overly influential role played by the
assemblies and the ruling class was not slow in appearing.

The master-mind behind it was Prince Andrew of Suzdal, who, when he became Grand Prince, went to Vladimir instead of Kiev. He ruled there from 1157-74, but was assassinated by boyars who were discontent with his despotism.

After the Mongol invasion (1238-40) and the destruction of the old Russian capital, Kiev, the center of activity was transferred to the north-east, to the region of Suzdal. There the landed princes ruled as autocrats in the new cities without sharing their power with the assemblies. By the beginning of the fourteenth century, there were three political centers in northern Russia: Novgorod the Great, which had kept the privilege of a free city where the prince only played a secondary role; Rostov the Great, where a duly-elected prince ruled along with the boyars and an assembly; and last, but not least, Moscow, a city whose importance was growing rapidly due to its exceptional princes, who were firm' believers in autocracy and the unification of the country.

Novgorod, which had been protected from the Mongol destruction by its geographical location, had a totally original constitution. It was a city-state, with numerous colonies and borders extending to the extreme north and north-west of the country. Founded as a commercial city around 700, it always maintained relations with the West, acting as an influential member of the Hanseatic League. It was governed by an assembly of the people who were called together in Saint Sophia Square by the sound of a bell. Although the Assembly was originally convened by the Prince, this duty later fell to the head of the government (*posadnik*) and to the archbishop. The assembly appointed and dismissed princes, elected and removed magistrates, met as a high court of justice, concluded treaties and declared war. Besides the assembly, there was also the governmental council, which was made up of the archbishop who was its head, the former heads of government (*posadniki*) and the provosts. Not only did the archbishop preside over the council, which met in his apartments, but he also exercised the right of veto (by refusing to give his blessing) on all governmental decisions. He placed his seal on all official documents and kept the archives and state treasury. He defended outsiders in their conflicts with the authorities and mediated all disputes. He was elected in a rather peculiar manner: the assembly proposed three names

55

from which one was drawn by lot. (P. Kovalesky, *Manuel de l'histoire russe*, Paris: Payot, 1948.) Novgorod was not only an important commercial center, but after Kiev, it was the greatest cultural center in Russia. Along with Rostov, it played a role of prime importance in the "Russian Renaissance" of the fourteenth century.

The second factor which weighed heavily on fourteenth-century Russia was the Mongol yoke. The Tartar invasions, which followed each other in rapid succession without leading to permanent occupation, caused the ruin of the country, as well as the exodus of citizens from the most exposed regions, which were also the richest in Russia. Certain unscrupulous princes incorporated the Mongols into the affairs of the country and ignored their calumnies in exchange for the right to rule. Thus, one of the first princes of Moscow, Yuri (George), had his opponent, Prince Michael of Tver, taken into captivity by the Mongols, where he died as a martyr.

Mongol influence on Russian life and ideas has been grossly exaggerated. For example, the practice of segregating women does not reflect the adoption of an Eastern custom, but rather the necessity to protect the women from being

abducted by the Tartars who were infesting the land. But if the eastern political and social influences were limited, the moral consequences of the Mongol yoke were extremely profound. In his book *The Saints of Ancient Russia* (Paris: YMCA, 1931; in Russian), G. Fedotov depicts in the following manner the situation in Russia at the beginning of the fourteenth century: "The first century of the Mongol yoke not only led to the destruction of the life of the state and the culture of ancient Russia, but it also suffocated the spiritual life for a long time. This is quite contrary to the notion that political and social catastrophe usually lead to a religious revival. There was definitely a religious reaction to the Russian predicament. The contemporary prophets saw the atrocities of the Tartar yoke as divine punishment for the people's sins. However, the material distress and the length of the struggle for life were so great that general degradation was the natural result of it. After more than a century, the Russian Church had no more new holy monks. The only canonized sanctity was that of the social action of the princes and in part of the bishops."

Nevertheless, the Church was in a privileged position.

Rostov the Great.

The Mongols were not yet Muslims and displayed a great tolerance towards Christians. Churches were exempt from paying tribute, and the metropolitans received certain privileges from the khans. As a result of this, the bishops and the heads of the Russian Church, the metropolitans of Kiev, increased in importance. They were the native protectors and the unifiers of the country. At the time of the dissolution of princely power and the division of Russia into little independent states, the metropolitan preserved a certain unity of the state. In the fourteenth century, it was he who, by virtue of his protection of the principality of Moscow, decided the future of the country. Saint Sergius, whose family was from Rostov, and despite the opposition between Rostov and Moscow, allied himself with the latter, anticipating the great historical role Moscow would play in the unification of the country and in the struggle against the Mongols.

Rostov the Great, the birthplace of Saint Sergius, was one of the oldest cities in Russia. An important free city from the eighth century, with a native Finnish population as well as a Slavic element, it kept its pagan traditions for a long time. Consequently, Christianity was introduced rather late. Rostov, which was peaceably taken over in the tenth century by Novgorod, which established there a popular assembly, became the religious capital of northeastern Russia in the eleventh century. The first Greek missionaries had to leave, and it was not until the second half of the eleventh century that the country was evangelized, through the apostolic effort of Saint Leontius, a former monk of the Monastery of the Caves in Kiev and a student of Saint Theodosius. Saint Leontius died in 1073 as a martyr at the hands of the pagan sages. In the service dedicated to him, the Church proclaims: "The Roman lands glorify Saints Peter and Paul; the Greek, Emperor Constantine; Kiev, Prince Vladimir; and Rostov glorifies you, O great Bishop Leontius, who performed an apostolic labor." The process of Christianization continued under Saint Isaiah, also a student of Saint Theodosius and bishop from 1078 to 1090, but the last vestiges of paganism were not destroyed until the time of the monk Abraham, founder of the Monastery of the Theophany. Rostov could, from the thirteenth century on, pride itself on an exceptionally rich school and library. The school, founded by Prince

58

Constantine in the monastery of Saint Gregory Nazianzen, possessed at the beginning of the fourteenth century more than 1,000 Greek and Slavic manuscripts. It was one of the cultural centers of northern Russia.

The city itself did not suffer much from the Mongol invasion, but the surrounding region was devastated and the young prince Vassilko was killed while fighting the Tartars. In 1262, the city rose up against the invaders, but it was still obliged to pay tribute. The brilliant epoch for Rostov the Great began with the reign of princes Boris and Gleb (1277). The latter fought against the Yasaks with the Tartars, married a relative of the khan and brought her to Christianity. Because of his influence with the Mongols, he freed many prisoners, received rights for his subjects and protected them against the exactions of the Asiatics. He built churches, exhibited great charity and benevolence and remained for the citizens of Rostov a symbol of the greatness of their city.

For a long time, Rostov fought for supremacy in the north-east against the new cities: Vladimir, Yaroslav and Suzdal, but this struggle was limited to questions of precedence. No one questioned Rostov's right to independence until the small neighboring principality of Moscow entered the competition. It eventually annexed Rostov, which lost its independence but remained for a long time an important religious and cultural center.

Moscow was a small market-town, mentioned for the first time in 1147 and destroyed by the Tartars in 1238. The principality began to grow and take on importance in the second half of the thirteenth century, under Prince Daniel and his son George. However, the real founder of Moscow's power was Daniel's second son, John, known as "money-bags" (1270-1341). The reasons for the rapid rise of Moscow were multiple. Its geographical situation at the intersection of the great routes from the East and West was exceptional. The politics of the princes attracted to their lands refugees from the South, by providing them with a relatively peaceful life, and because the princes knew how to manage the Tartars, their policies were also important in this respect. However, the decisive factor was the establishment of Moscow as the religious center of all Russia. As early as the end of the thirteenth century, the metropolitans had left Kiev, which had

59

been totally ruined, and went to live in Vladimir. At the beginning of the fourteenth century (1325), Metropolitan Peter established his throne in Moscow and built the Cathedral of the Dormition, which became the main cathedral of all Russia. In the period which we will be studying, we see Rostov the Great submitted to its little neighbor Moscow, which in turn became the center of the Russian lands. This work of unification, which was pursued with great intensity, drew so heavily upon the material energies of the new principality that it was to the detriment of its spiritual needs. The life and work of Saint Sergius were dedicated to providing this spiritual nourishment.

THE SOURCES

We possess two documents of prime importance on the life of Saint Sergius which date from the first half of the fifteenth century. These documents, which do not tell much of the experiences of his youth, should be augmented by the local chronicles, which are especially informative in this area. Of the two "lives" which have come down to us, the first is the most precious. It was written by Epiphanius the Wise, a monk of the Trinity Lavra and a student of Saint Sergius. It dates from the years 1417-18 and was written twenty-five years after Saint Sergius' death. The other "Life" is ascribed to the Serbian scholar Pachomius the Logothete and is dated 1440-1443.

Epiphanius the Wise was a learned man who had a remarkable knowledge of the Holy Scriptures, the Church Fathers and Slavic hagiographic literature, and was not without literary talent. He had been a disciple of Saint Stephen of Perm at the school of Saint Gregory Nazianzen in Rostov and entered the Trinity Lavra after the great missionary left to evangelize the Zyrians in 1379. The "Lives" of Saint Sergius and of Saint Stephen which he wrote are long, amply replete with scriptural passages and accounts of peripheral episodes. Despite its length, the life of Saint Sergius is particularly important because it provides us with many details on the daily life of the monastery and is full of personal

Epiphanius questions witnesses of Saint Sergius' life.

observations. For twelve years, Epiphanius lived close to Saint Sergius and for more than twenty years he collected materials for his "Life," which ends with the death of the saint. Epiphanius brings out the humility, mercy and monastic poverty of Saint Sergius, but he is markedly reserved in speaking about his national actions. One is inclined to feel that Epiphanius was sympathetic to Rostov and opposed to the pretentions of Moscow.

Pachomius the Logothete abridged Epiphanius' text, deleted the anti-Muscovite tendencies and deprived it of its most precious element: those characteristic features of the era and his personal observations. In Russia, Pachomius was the most illustrious representative of the "artificial" hagiographic literature which transformed the actual lives of the saints into panegyrics applicable to any saint, since it omitted any specific characteristics which did not fit the already established schema. This type of "Life" was introduced in the East by Simeon Metaphrastes and arrived in Russia through Pachomius. In addition to the life of Saint Sergius, he wrote those of Saint Alexis, Metropolitan of all Russia, and Saint Nikon, friend and successor of Saint Sergius as the head of the monastery. He also wrote several famous chronicles. He was a firm supporter of the unification of Russia under the scepter of the Muscovite princes.

Using the life written by Epiphanius as a basis, Pachomius added to his version accounts of miracles and his canonization, but omitted any mention of the flight of Saint Sergius' parents from the Muscovite governors as well as any details of his life in the forest. According to Pachomius, Saint Sergius gave all of his possessions to the poor, although we know that he gave them to his younger brother Peter. Pachomius also portrayed the animals which surrounded Sergius in the forest as demons tempting him. His departure after the arrival of his eldest brother Stephen is ascribed to his desire to return to the calm of the desert, whereas it was actually because he was so humble that he did not want to contradict his elder brother. Despite its defects, the "Life" written by Pachomius soon became the official record. We will employ both lives, adding details from various chronicles of the era and other saints' lives. There are many manuscripts of the numerous Russian editions. The most famous manuscript of the "Life" of Saint Sergius, which dates from the sixteenth century, is decorated with approximately 300 color miniatures. Originally kept at the Trinity Lavra, it is now kept in the public library of Moscow. Some of its miniatures are reproduced here through the kindness of the administration of the Moscow library.

FAMILY, BACKGROUND, BIRTH AND YOUTH

Saint Sergius came from a family of rich boyars from Rostov the Great. They owned land not far from the city. By the time of his birth, they were poor. The Tartar invasions, the payment of tribute and the years of bad harvest reduced their fortune so that they possessed only the products of their own lands. Cyril and Mary were pious and wise. Their house, like most lordly Russian homes in this era, did not resemble a palace in any way. It was a large, wooden country house, surrounded by meadows and gardens.` Fires destroyed almost all of the old houses of northern Russia, but those which survive or have been reconstructed show an exquisite taste in the choice of wooden ornaments for various parts of the' house. Although these houses were simple, each owner, be he lord or peasant, added something reflecting his personal taste.

Saint Sergius' father, as the confidant of the prince of Rostov, accompanied him on his journeys throughout the Mongol Horde. The principality of Rostov was undergoing a critical period: Mongol bands had invaded it several times and it was necessary to negotiate not only with the individual chiefs but with the Horde and to seek protection and a guarantee of rights from the khan. The inhabitants of Rostov already had the experience of parleys with the Tartars. Bishop Cyril (1231-62) was one of the first to go to the Golden Horde, beyond the Volga, in order to defend his city. He brought back a Tartar prince whom he had converted to Christianity. The prince was the founder of the monastery of Saint Peter (near Rostov), where he was buried. Later, Prince Gleb of Rostov married a Tartar princess who took the name Theodora. Negotiations with the Horde were very difficult, but

Rostov also felt itself threatened from another side. Because Rostov was weak, the princes of Moscow were planning to annex it. Prince Basil was the last independent ruler of Rostov. His sons, Theodore and Constantine, lost their inheritance to Moscow.

The land of Saint Sergius' parents was called "Varnitsa," which means "salt mines." Owners of salt works probably named the area. Cyril and Mary led a simple life and showed a warm hospitality. They had three sons: the eldest was named Stephen, the second was Bartholomew and the third, Peter.

The "Lives" do not give the year of Saint Sergius' birth, but from his age at his death (he died in 1392 at the age of 78), one can assume that he was born in 1313-1314.[3] Biographers often emphasize the miracles surrounding his birth. His parents, like all Russians of their time, had a small family chapel[4] where they prayed twice daily with their children and servants. On Sundays and feasts they went to the churches of Rostov and the surrounding monasteries. One Sunday, while still pregnant with her second child, Saint Ser-

The cry of the infant in his mother's womb.

gius' mother attended the Liturgy. As she stood with the other women before the reading from the Gospel, there was a cry. The women near her turned around, but no one really paid attention. It is quite common to hear babies crying in Orthodox churches, since they are brought to church from the time of their baptism. A louder cry was heard before the Cherubic Hymn and an even louder one before the priest's communion. The mother, hearing the child crying in her womb, was frightened and almost fainted. The women around her wanted to calm her, but she had to confess that the child was not yet born. This extraordinary sign impressed everyone present. The mother spoke with her husband and promised to consecrate the child to God.

The child was born on May 3, the day of Saint Theodosius of Kiev. The baby refused its mother's milk on the days on which she had eaten meat and she decided to abstain from it. On the fortieth day, she went to be churched and the priest baptized the child, naming him Bartholomew, in honor of the apostle whose feast was that day.[5] The parents told the priest, Father Michael, about the extraordinary events which had

The priest's predictions of Bartholomew's sanctity.

preceded the birth of their son. He then told them: "Rejoice, for your child will be a chosen vessel of God and a servant of the Holy Trinity."

We know almost nothing of the life of the young Bartholomew until he was seven years old. He led the life of a country lad, going to Rostov and on a pilgrimage to the various monasteries in the area with his parents and helping them with domestic work. From his childhood he grew accustomed to solitude, for he used to tend the horses while they were in the meadows.

When Bartholomew reached the age of seven, his parents sent him to school to learn to read and write, but his studies did not interest him. He preferred wandering in the fields and meadows to working with his schoolmates. His parents and teacher scolded him, but the call of nature and solitude was stronger than their injunctions. The area surrounding Rostov was full of a "calm beauty." Little forests of birch trees alternated with meadows descending to Lake Nero, on the banks of which the city and several monasteries were located. There were not vast expanses or horizons as in southern Russia, but the area was pleasant and calm. The fortress (*kremlin*) of Rostov the Great, a bustling commercial city, was surrounded by "a white enclosure with ten towers and included the residences of the prince and the bishop as well as several churches. All around were suburbs which resembled villages more than parts of a city."[6]

The "Life" depicts Saint Sergius' school-days in the following manner: "At age seven, his parents sent him to school to learn how to read and write. The servant of God, Cyril, had three sons: the first, Stephen, the second, Bartholomew, and the third, Peter. They were all firmly raised in piety and chastity. Stephen and Peter learned reading and writing quickly, but Bartholomew had problems. Not only did he learn slowly, but he was also unable to apply himself to his work. His teacher taught him with great care, but Bartholomew did not heed his words nor could he come to understand them. He was not as clever as his classmates. He was scolded much by his parents and suffered a great deal because his teacher and fellow students always reprimanded him."

Bartholomew prayed ceaselessly that God would enable him to read and understand books. One day, his father sent

Appearance of the monk (angel) to Bartholomew.

him to bring back some stray horses. In a clearing he saw an old monk praying under an oak. Bartholomew approached him. When the old man had finished his prayers, he asked Bartholomew whence he came and what he wanted. The young man told him about his life and his problems. The monk listened to him, prayed, and gave him a little piece of

67

prosphora[7] which he had in his bag, saying: "Take and eat: this is given to you as a sign of the divine grace for reading. From this day on you will exceed your brothers and friends in your studies." Although the old monk spoke at great length with him, the rest of the conversation is unknown. Bartholomew invited the old man to his house, where he was received with great honor. Before eating, he went to the chapel and asked Bartholomew to follow him. There he told him to read the Hours; he answered that he could not read, but the monk repeated his order and added: "I have already told you that from this day on God will give you understanding of whatever you read." Then, to the surprise of all, Bartholomew started reading the Hours.

During the meal, the parents asked the old man about their son. They said: "We are afraid and do not know what to think. What will our child become?" "You need not be

The monk (angel) is welcomed at the home of Bartholomew's parents.

afraid," said the monk, "but you should rejoice because this young man will be great before God and men because of his virtuous life. He will be a servant of the Holy Trinity." With these words, the old man left the house and was never seen again.

No one knew who he was and local legends explained the visit in a different way. The "Life," with its exquisite discretion, only mentions the question which the parents raised: "Was this not an angel who was sent to give our son the ability to read?" Under the porch of the monastery of Varnitsa, built in 1480 on the site of the house of Saint Sergius' parents (or according to other local legends, the place where the old man appeared to Bartholomew), there was a painting portraying the miraculous meeting with the following inscription: "This monastery is founded on the spot where an angel of God appeared as an old monk to Bartholomew, who was later Sergius, the wonder-worker of Radonezh and the founder of the great Lavra." Another legend claims that it was Saint Abraham of Rostov who, along with Saint Theodosius of Kiev, served as an example for Saint Sergius in his monastic life. With a remarkable sobriety, the "Life" concludes the account of the monk's visit in the following manner: "After the departure of this old man, Bartholomew found that he could read everything and he changed radically. No matter what book he opened, he could read well and understand it."

From that time, Bartholomew began to read the Bible and liturgical books and soon he was reading the Church Fathers, whose works he could find in the Rostov library. Nevertheless, throughout his life he remained a man for whom the Christian experience was more important than learning or reason. He never wrote anything, and he drew his knowledge not from reading but from his continual communion with God. His vocation was not to speculative theology but rather to the application of the Gospel's precepts to life. He was always serene and moderate in all things, modest and poor, and an example to all those around him. He would not leave his parents despite the call of solitude.

His parents knew that he was chosen by God, but his mother worried about his ascetical practices and pleaded with him to not develop an overly rigorous discipline. For Saint

Sergius, this life of prayer, fasting and work was completely natural and he never fell into excess. Everything was harmonious and calm in their family, which was a real Christian unity. The parents never pushed their son, and he was always obedient, awaiting the moment when he could answer the Lord's call.

Bartholomew often attended services in the churches of Rostov, in the monastery of Saint Gregory Nazianzen and in the three lavras in the area. The cathedral of Rostov the Great was dedicated to the Dormition of the Theotokos.[8] According to local chronicles, it was founded in 997, during the days of Saint Vladimir, but was burned in 1160 in a fire which destroyed the city. Rebuilt by Prince Andrew in 1213, it collapsed and was not rebuilt until 1230-31 when Prince Constantine the Wise and Bishop Cyril reconstructed it. The cathedral holds the relics of the apostles of the area, Saint Leontius, Saint Isaiah and Prince Vassilko. Especially attractive for pilgrims was the icon of the Theotokos which was painted in the eleventh century by Saint Alypius of Kiev. Next to the cathedral were the churches of Saint John the Apostle and of Our Lady, Joy of All the Afflicted, as well as the monastery of Saint Gregory Nazianzen with its famous library and school.

In the immediate vicinity of Rostov there were three lavras which Bartholomew visited. He took an active part in the services, reading and singing in the choir. The Monastery of the Savior was founded in 1238 by the widow of Prince Vassilko of Rostov, who had been killed by the Mongols while protecting the city. The princess became a nun and was buried there along with her son, Prince Gleb. This monastery was built on the shore of Lake Nero.

When Bishop Cyril returned from the Golden Horde in 1246,[9] he brought back a Tartar prince whom he baptized and named Peter. The princes of Rostov offered their guest land not far from the city, and it was there that the widower-prince built the lavra of Saint Peter the Apostle in honor of his patron saint. Having himself become a monk and after leading a life of humility and piety, he died on June 29, 1290, and was canonized by the Russian Church. Bartholomew often went to the lavra of Saint Peter, near the tomb of

The young Bartholomew reads and chants in church.

71

the saint "who loved silence and meditation" and prayed before the icons of the Mother of God, Saint Nicholas and Saint Demetrius of Thessalonica, who had all appeared to Prince Peter.

Bartholomew was especially attracted to the old lavra of the Theophany, which was probably founded at the end of the eleventh century by Saint Abraham of Rostov. His life is unfortunately cluttered by apocryphal tales. However we can trust the details of his daily life and the description of his virtues, which alone were important to Bartholomew. The account of Saint Abraham's ascetical labors was current in Rostov at the time of Saint Sergius, and the monastery still kept the traditions inaugurated by its founder.

Saint Abraham probably arrived in Rostov at the end of the eleventh century. He built a hut on the shores of Lake Nero and fought for years against the remnants of paganism. It is said that he destroyed the last idol with a stick given to him in a dream by Saint John the Theologian. Saint Abraham founded the lavra of the Theophany on the site of the destruction of the last idol and built a church dedicated to Saint John the Theologian on the spot where he appeared to him. It became the parish church of the village of Bogoslovskoye ("of the Theologian"), three miles from Rostov. After he became abbot of the monastery, Saint Abraham continued to work like a simple monk, serving as an example of humility, poverty and charity. He was canonized and his relics were offered for veneration under Prince Vsevolod at the end of the twelfth century. Thus, at the age of fourteen, Bartholomew already had a personal experience of prayer and the excellent example of saints such as Saint Abraham and Saint Theodosius of Kiev to guide him in his preparation for the monastic life.

DEPARTURE FROM ROSTOV—THE DEATH OF HIS PARENTS AND THE DESERT

After the death of Prince Basil, who had loved Cyril, Bartholomew's father, the principality was divided between his two sons, Theodore and Constantine. The latter married the daughter of the Prince of Moscow, John I, who decided to annex his lands to Moscow. John I, surnamed "Money-bags" (Kalita) because of his extremes of thriftiness, was an extremely able ruler and an excellent administrator. He attracted to the city the head of the Russian Church, Metropolitan Peter, who transferred his see there and blessed the foundation of the Cathedral of the Dormition.

In 1328, Prince John I of Moscow became Grand Prince of Russia and immediately put into action his plan for annexing Rostov. The city could not resist its powerful neighbor, who installed two governors with extensive powers. One was Basil, surnamed "Kocheva" ("nomad"), and the other Mina. These two representatives of the Grand Prince oppressed the people and set out against the nobility of Rostov, whom they saw as a class opposed to the authoritarian regime of Moscow. The most highly placed families were forced to leave the principality. Moscow, which was beginning an autocratic reign everywhere, could not tolerate a free city with a powerful class of boyars. Nevertheless, Rostov, despite its political decline, remained a religious and cultural center and played a great role in Russian life until the era of Peter the Great.

Officials from Moscow oppressing the inhabitants of Rostov.

Bartholomew and his relatives.

The "Life" of Saint Sergius relates in the following way the events of 1388: "It was an unfortunate year for the city of Rostov, and especially for its princes, because their power was taken away. Their principalities, their goods, their honor, their glory—all passed on to Moscow." But next to this description of the misfortune of Rostov, we find in a Muscovite chronicle a different picture of this same period: "Under John Kalita, great peace began, and the pagans stopped fighting Russia and killing the Christians, and the Christians rested from their pain and from their great torment." (*Complete Collection of Chronicles*, vol. 18, p. 90.) Despite his attachment to Rostov, Saint Sergius supported the "uniters of the Russian land," the princes of Moscow who dared to face the Tartars and react against the fratricidal wars which had been tearing the country apart.

At Radonezh.

Bartholomew's parents, like other noble families of Rostov, were obliged to seek refuge in this very principality of Moscow, which had become the only island of peace in the midst of the turbulent states which surrounded it. Cyril and Mary and their three children settled in the little town of Radonezh, 160 kilometers south of Rostov and some 60 kilometers northeast of Moscow.[10] This town belonged to the son of John of Moscow, Andrew, who was still a minor. His father sent as governor a man who in no way resembled the two tyrants who terrorized Rostov. Terence Rtischa promised lands and privileges to those who settled in the area. In his "Life," Epiphanius the Wise gives a list of those who, along with Bartholomew's parents, settled in Radonezh.

Cyril and Mary had brought some of their goods with them and settled near the Church of the Nativity of the Holy

75

Virgin, which became their parish church. Their eldest son, Stephen, who was already married and had two sons, Clement and John, the future Archbishop of Rostov, went to work for the young prince. Cyril was too old for this and spent his time working with his new property. Peter was also married, but Bartholomew remained alone with his parents. He asked them to let him leave for the desert, but his father insisted that he stay near them. "We are old and sick and have no one to take care of us. Your brothers have their families to feed. We are happy to have a son who is devoted to God, but your vocation will remain intact if you stay with us until God calls us to Himself. See us to our graves and no one will keep you from following your vocation."

Bartholomew consented to remain near his parents. They decided to enter a neighboring monastery in Khotkovo, where there were two communities, one for men and one for women. There they died peacefully in 1334, six years after their arrival in Radonezh. Their eldest son Stephen, who had become a widower, went to the same monastery. Then Bartholomew had only to arrange his estate. He stayed forty days in Khotkovo, near the graves of his parents, then sold all of his possessions and left his share of his father's will to his younger brother Peter and decided to leave for the desert. He asked his brother Stephen if he would like to share his life there. He agreed, and leaving the world they went north into the forests of Radonezh. One can ask if, in his decision to have his elder brother with him during the years of testing, he had a desire for submission. Bartholomew was only twenty years old and not yet a monk. He wanted to live under the guidance of a shepherd who was not only his elder brother, but who had also already taken the monastic habit.

The brothers chose to found their hermitage in a razed clearing, not far from a little river. It was surrounded by fir trees and old pines and was called "Makovitsa" ("the fruit of the poppy," a term often used to indicate the top of a hill). They decided to build a chapel and a cell there. The place was ten miles away from any village, and there was no road leading to it. Before beginning their work, they went to Moscow and asked Metropolitan Theognostus (1328-1353) to bless them to establish a church. He received them with charity and authorized them to build a chapel where they could sing the offices and pray, waiting till a priest could celebrate the Liturgy there.

Everywhere there was wood in abundance, but it was necessary to be able to handle an axe and other tools. The brothers set to work sawing and pulling down trees and carrying the trunks to the clearing. Working as carpenters, they remembered the youth of Christ who helped Joseph. We know that Saint Sergius was an able worker and that he later built a cell for one of his companions.

The question arose of the patron saint of their church. Although Bartholomew venerated the Theotokos, and Stephen was a monk of the monastery of the Nativity of the Mother of God, they named their church for the Holy Trinity. The elder brother remembered the prediction of the priest Michael and that of the old monk. Both had foretold that some day the child would be a servant of the Trinity. When the chapel was finished, Metropolitan Theognostus sent a priest to consecrate the church. It is possible that this was the abbot Metrophanes, future co-worker with Saint Sergius. He visited

Bartholomew and Stephen build a chapel in the forest.

the hermits from time to time to serve in their chapel and to give them Holy Communion.

We know very little about the life of Stephen and Bartholomew in the forests of Radonezh. It was very difficult and required a good deal of perseverance and will. The elder brother could not take the rigors of winter and the scarcity of food. He left Bartholomew for an urban monastery and went to live in the Lavra of the Theophany. It was founded in 1296 by Prince Daniel and developed by John Kalita in 1304. At that time it was the only organized monastery in Moscow. There he found, in his novitiate, Alexis, the future Metropolitan of Moscow, with whom he established a close friendship. They sang together and led an exemplary life of prayer and fasting. Metropolitan Theognostus ordained Stephen to the priesthood and made him the head of the monastery. The Grand Prince made him the court chaplain. While remaining an excellent monk, Stephen preferred life in an urban monastery. On the other hand, Bartholomew restored the solitary monastic life in the north. If in Kievan Russia almost all of the monasteries were built in the middle of cities or near them, those in the north were almost all withdrawn from the world, far from any human life: in the forest, on islands, and later even beyond the polar circle. Bartholomew remained alone in the "desert," and in silence and prayer he prepared himself for his monastic vows. The "Life" speaks of him in these terms, "Our father, like Christ," was not yet a monk, and had not yet studied those things pertaining to monastic life."

LIFE IN THE FOREST—FIRST COMPANIONS

In the third year of his life as a hermit, Bartholomew asked Abbot Metrophanes, who visited from time to time, to set him apart as a monk. This took place on October 7, 1337, the feast of the holy martyrs Sergius and Bacchus. The abbot named him Sergius. He was twenty-three years old at that time. The "Life" describes the event in the following manner: "He called to his desert Abbot Metrophanes and asked him, with humility, bowing deeply before him, 'My father,

Bartholomew, tonsured as a monk by Metrophanes, takes the name Sergius.

78

show charity to me and let me enter the monastic state. I have desired it since my youth, but the pleas of my parents held me back. Now, my lord and father, I am free and I thirst for living water (Ps. 42).' The abbot immediately entered the church and received him as a monk."

The young monk received Communion and as the "Life" recounts, the air of the church was heavily scented. Saint Sergius remained in the church seven days, eating only the prosphora he had received from the hands of the abbot. He sang the Psalms. Before the old monk left, Sergius said to him with great humility, "Bless me, a humble monk, and pray for my solitary life. Instruct me in how I should live alone in the desert and how I should pray to the Lord and how to resist the Enemy and his proud thoughts, for I am inexperienced and have just become a monk."

The monk instructed him and left him alone in the desert. We do not know how long Saint Sergius lived alone in the forests of Radonezh. Epiphanius says in his "Life" that only God knows how long. The young monk was in solitude. His

life was difficult and the temptations many. The beasts surrounded him, nature was inclement, the winters severe, and it was difficult to find food. Several times hungry wolves surrounded his cell and bears came to his dwelling. All hermits had to struggle against temptations and the attacks of the devil. Epiphanius tells us of two terrifying visions: "Once Sergius entered the cell in the night to sing Matins. When he began to sing, the wall of the church suddenly opened and the Devil entered, accompanied by a multitude of his servants. They attacked the blessed one, grinding their teeth and taunting him, 'Flee from this place or we will destroy you and you will die at our hands.' Armed with prayer, the saint said in a loud voice, 'Let God arise and let His enemies be scattered,' and the demons disappeared." Another time, when he was in his cell praying during the night, he heard a noise, and again a multitude of demons attacked him, crying, "Go away. Why did you come to this desert? Leave as soon as possible or we will kill you." The saint prayed, and divine strength illumined him and chased the demons away. All of Saint Sergius' temptations were frightening. The temptations of the flesh, frequent among the Egyptian hermits, never touched him. Saint Sergius' life was always poor, simple, moderate, and all the distractions of the world were foreign to him.

Epiphanius relates an incident which shows the saint's charity, even towards wild beasts. "Many wild beasts lived in this desert. Some were distant and others approached the blessed one. A bear came to his house every day. Seeing that the animal came not out of wickedness but to receive something to eat, the saint brought a loaf of bread and put it on a tree stump. When the bear arrived, he found his meal, took it in his mouth, and left. When the bread was not there, the bear waited for his usual portion. Sergius did not have a variety of food, but only water from a spring and a little bit of bread. When he had no bread both he and the bear were left hungry. Sometimes when the blessed one only had one piece of bread, he gave it to the bear, not wishing to offend him or let him go away hungry."

Saint Sergius read and studied the Bible, worked in his garden, and spent most of his time praying. Epiphanius ex-

Saint Sergius feeds his bear.

plains in the following manner the arrival of his first companions in the desert. "The most extraordinary thing was that no one knew of his difficult and virtuous life. Only God, who sees everything which is hidden, knew of it. But later, seeing his great faith and patience, God had pity on him and wishing to ease his burden in the desert, He placed in the heart of several pious monks the idea of going to Sergius. The blessed one asked them, 'Can you bear the harshness of this place, the lack of food and drink, and all its privations?' They answered, 'Yes, venerable father, we desire it with the help of God and by your prayers.' Seeing their faith and zeal, Saint Sergius was surprised and said to them, 'Lords and brothers, I desire to live alone in this desert and to end my life in this place, but if God wishes that there be a monastery here, may His will be done. I receive you with joy, but set out to build cells. Know that if you have come to live in the desert, the beginning of all virtue must be the fear of God.' "

Despite the distance of the hermitage, word concerning the exemplary life of the hermit of Radonezh soon spread everywhere. Abbot Metrophanes, and perhaps other monks, came from time to time to visit him and bring him food. Among the first to come was an old monk named Basil, surnamed "the Dry," who came from the area of the Dubna River, and another monk named James. There was also a Deacon Onesimus and his father Eliseus. They built cells surrounded by a wooden wall, at whose door they placed a guard. Saint Sergius was still young and very strong and could work for two. He himself built four of the cells. Every day the monks came together in the church to sing Nocturn, Matins, the Hours, Vespers, and Compline. On Sundays and feast days, Saint Sergius invited the old Abbot Metrophanes to celebrate the Liturgy and give them Communion. He felt himself unworthy of the priesthood and did not wish to become abbot of the little monastery. He said that in the monastic life, the beginning of all evil is the pride which makes one want to be an abbot. The blessed one worked all day for his little monastery. He carried out the most difficult tasks, cutting the wood and bringing kindling for the kitchen. Epiphanius describes the birth of the lavra in this way, "The monastery was marvelous at this time. The forest was not as far away as it is now (1417), but where they built the cells, large trees shaded them. Around the church there were many tree stumps. Alongside it they planted different vegetables." Saint Sergius ground wheat, baked bread, prepared the food, made boots and habits for the monks, carried water from the spring and left a bucket at each monk's cell. He spent the night praying, eating only a little bread and water, and never spent an hour without working. The monks who lived in individual cells spent their time copying manuscripts or painting icons. The old Abbot Metrophanes later joined the community and became the first abbot. For a long time the number of Saint Sergius' companions was limited to twelve in commemoration of the twelve apostles of the Lord.

Construction of the Monastery of the Trinity.

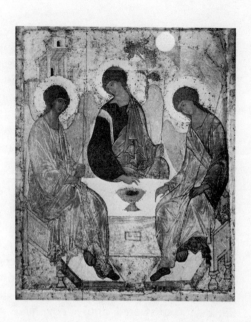

*Rublev's icon of
the Holy Trinity.*

SAINT SERGIUS: ABBOT OF
THE TRINITY LAVRA

Abbot Metrophanes only remained a year in the monastery. He fell ill and died. Then the brothers decided to elect Saint Sergius abbot of the community. They went to him and said, "Father, we cannot live without a superior. We want you to be our abbot and the guide of our souls and bodies." The blessed one said to them, "I never wanted to be an abbot, and my soul longs to finish my days here as a simple monk." The monks insisted and came three more times to Saint Sergius to persuade him to accept this responsibility. Then the blessed one said to them, "I would rather learn than teach, obey than command, but fearing the judgment of God, I submit myself to His will. May it be done." Saint Sergius decided to go to see his bishop and submit his case to him. He took his two oldest monks with him and set out on foot for Pereslav, "beyond the forests" (*Zalesky*), where Bishop Athanasius of Volynia (1328-1353) then resided. This bishop was filling the place of Metropolitan Theognostus, who was on a trip to Constantinople. The old metropolitan, who had given his blessing to the foundation of the monastery, was Greek by nationality, and had gone to see the Patriarch. The trip was long and dangerous, for he had to cross the southern steppes and set out from the only port open between Russia and Byzantium, Kaffa (now Theodosius) in the Crimea. Thus he could not leave the Church without a pastor.[12] According to the "Life," this took place in 1344.

Saint Sergius and the two monks arrived in the morning at Pereslav, located halfway between the monastery and Rostov, and went to the bishop, who received them with joy. He had heard of the community of the Trinity, and asked the monks to set their case before him. Saint Sergius recounted what had happened in his monastery and asked the bishop to give them a superior. The bishop interrupted him and said, "God called you from your mother's womb and you will be a superior of the monastery of the all-holy Trinity." The saint refused, saying he was unworthy of this responsibility, but the bishop answered him, "You have gained everything except obedience." Then the blessed one accepted, and the bishop led him to the church where he ordained him subdeacon and then, at the Divine Liturgy, deacon. The following day, Saint Sergius was ordained priest, and the bishop named him abbot. He charged him to sing the Divine Liturgy and to offer from his hands the bloodless sacrifice of the Eucharist. Then he called him into his cell, where he spoke with him at great length about his new responsibility and gave him the rules of the Desert Fathers for guiding souls.

The return of the newly ordained abbot to his monastery is described by Epiphanius in these words, "Our father and abbot Sergius returned to his monastery, the abode of the Holy Trinity, and the monks received him, prostrating themselves before him, but he immediately entered the church, prostrated himself before the icon of the Trinity, and prayed humbly. Only after praying did he address his brothers, saying, 'Enter by the narrow gate (Mt. 7:14). Come, my brothers, listen to me; I will teach you the fear of the eternal one (Ps. 34:11). Remember the words of the apostle Paul to the Galatians: The fruit of the spirit is love, joy, peace, patience, goodness, kindness, faithfulness, gentleness, and temperance'

Saint Sergius is ordained priest.

86

(Gal. 5:22-23)." Then he added, "Brethren, pray for me for I lack gentleness and wisdom, but I have received a talent from the king of heaven and I must account for it." Accepting his new responsibility as a prior, Saint Sergius did not change anything in his life and continued to work for all. He had kept and practiced the words which his bishop had addressed to him when he dismissed him, "Remember this saying: 'Bear one another's burdens and so fulfill the law of Christ' (Gal. 6:2). If you follow this precept, you will save

yourself and those who live with you." Saint Sergius remembered this all his life and was not only a father but also a servant to all those who came to him.

The number of monks remained at twelve. The "Life" says, "At the beginning of his time as abbot, there were twelve monks and the abbot was the thirteenth. This was so for two or three years. This number neither grew nor diminished, and if a brother died or left the monastery, another was taken so that the number always remained at twelve." A great change in the life of the monastery took place in 1347. A rich and famous abbot from Smolensk, named Simon, having heard of Saint Sergius arrived at the monastery and asked to be received as his disciple. It was difficult for the abbot to resolve this problem. First, Abbot Simon was an archimandrite,[13] a title given to the superiors of large monasteries, and should have taken precedence over him. In addition, he brought a large amount of money to Saint Sergius, who wanted his monastery to remain poor. The first problem was solved by the humility and great wisdom of Abbot Simon, who wished to remain a simple monk and follow the rule imposed by the community. As for the money, they unanimously decided to use it for building a new church, the old one having become too small.

The arrival of Archimandrite Simon had another effect which the saint could not foresee. Once the number of twelve monks was surpassed, they could not stop the arrival of new candidates, and the community began to grow in a disturbing manner. The saint refused no one the right to enter the monastery, but he did not make the candidate a monk. To begin with, he ordered them to wear dark clothing and to live with the brothers in order to grow accustomed little by little to the monastic rule. Then he heard their first vows and did not let them make their final vows until after a certain time had passed.

Epiphanius writes, "From the beginning, Saint Sergius followed this practice. After Vespers, late in the evening, and especially during the long and dark nights, he left his cell and visited the cells of the monks. If he saw that the monk was praying or working, he rejoiced and thanked God. If he saw two or three monks talking and laughing together,

Archimandrite Simon arrives at the Trinity Monastery.

Saint Sergius tours the monks' cells.

he became indignant, and having knocked on the window, he
continued on his way. In the morning he called them and
'from a distance' instructed them by parables, with humility
and gentleness. If the monk were humble and obedient, he
recognized his error, bowed before the abbot, and asked his
pardon. If he were not obedient and remained insensitive, as
though what the superior was saying did not concern him,
then the abbot admonished him with patience and gave him
a penance. Thus he taught all of them to pray intensely and
not to talk after evening prayers, but to work according to
their abilities, singing the Psalms throughout the day."

Among the first arrivals was the older brother of Saint
Sergius, Abbot Stephen, his first companion in solitude, who,
after a stay in Moscow, decided to return to the Trinity
Lavra. He brought with him his twelve-year-old son John,
who became a monk under the name of Theodore. From his

90

Saint Sergius makes bread and candles.

childhood, this youth was very pious and obedient, always
following the example of his uncle.

After becoming abbot, Saint Sergius changed nothing in
the life of the community. He followed the rule of Saint
Theodosius of Kiev, but he relaxed it, replacing rigid require-
ments with gentleness and humility. He said that any rule
should be as an educational tool in the hands of the abbot,
who should know how to apply it according to the abilities
of each individual monk. For him the monastic life was a
school and the abbot a teacher who helped his brothers to
progress in the way of the Gospel. Saint Sergius officiated
every day, and he himself prepared the prosphora, grinding
the wheat and making the dough. He also made the candles.
As before, he worked for everyone, dressing poorly and giving to all an example of humility and work.

The growth in the number of monks was accompanied

by another difficulty for the saint. Many lay people, farmers and city dwellers, leaving their villages and towns, came from all over to settle in the area of the Trinity Lavra. The "Life" says, "They began to chop down the forests and no one forbade them from doing so. They built houses and thus stripped the forests. They did not spare the wilderness, and turned the forests into a wasteland, as we now see it. They built villages and farms and began to visit the monastery, bringing countless gifts with them.

"The poverty of the monastery had been extreme up until that time. The monks often lacked bread and meal or wine, incense and beeswax. They sang Matins at night without candles, burning embers of birch or pine. One day, the abbot had no bread or salt, and the entire monastery was without food. However Saint Sergius had forbidden the brothers to go out begging. They all had to remain in the monastery and wait for help from God. The abbot spent three days without eating and on the morning of the fourth day, he went with his axe to one of the monks, named Daniel, and said, 'I have heard that you wish to build a room in front of your cell. I have come to build this antechamber for you, so that my hands will not be idle.' Daniel answered him, 'Yes, I have wanted it for a long time.' 'I will not ask much in return,' said the saint. 'Don't you have a piece of mouldy bread? I would like very much to eat it, and I will not ask anything else of you. You will find no other carpenter like me.' The monk brought him a bowl of mouldy bread, saying, 'This is all that I have.' Saint Sergius answered, 'This is fine with me, but hide it until the Ninth Hour, for I do not want to receive my pay before having finished my work.' In the evening, when all the work was done, the old Daniel brought him the bowl and the abbot ate this mouldy bread with some water, because there was neither soup nor salt in the monastery."

DISSATISFACTION AMONG THE MONKS—
FIRST MIRACLES

Once the monastery was without bread for two days, and some of the monks went to the abbot and requested his permission to go ask for bread in the neighboring villages: "We have followed you, we have obeyed your orders, but tomorrow we will go to look for food. We will not return because we cannot bear the poverty and lack of food in this place." The abbot then gathered all of the monks and admonished them with words of the Bible. Quoting the Gospel, he reproached them for their lack of faith: "Therefore I tell you, do not be anxious about your life, what you shall eat or what you shall drink, nor about your body, what you shall put on. Is not life more than food, and the body more than clothing? Look at the birds of the air. They neither sow nor reap nor gather into barns, and yet your heavenly Father feeds them. Are you not of more value than they?" (Matt. 7:25-26). He told them that they had to endure this test. "Joy will soon replace your sorrows. Although you now do not have any bread, tomorrow God will give you all that you need. The Lord will not forget this holy place and those who live in it." The "Life" continues: "As he was talking, someone knocked on the door. The gate-keeper looked through the opening and saw a cart full of food. He was so surprised that he did not open the gate but ran instead to the abbot: 'Father, someone has brought bread and food, by your prayers, and all of this is now at the gate.' Then Saint Sergius ordered them to open the gate and receive the goods." Two full carts entered, and Saint Sergius invited those who had brought them to join them for a meal. He did not eat anything, but went instead to thank God. Only after giving thanks did he bless the breads and distribute them to the entire community. Epiphanius states that "the breads were fresh and tasted as though they had been made of butter and honey." The abbot then asked those who had brought the food whence they came. They told him that a wealthy servant of God who lived far away had asked them to bring these breads to Saint Sergius and his monks. They declined his offer to eat with the monks and said that they still had work to do. On the two days following, large quantities of food continued to

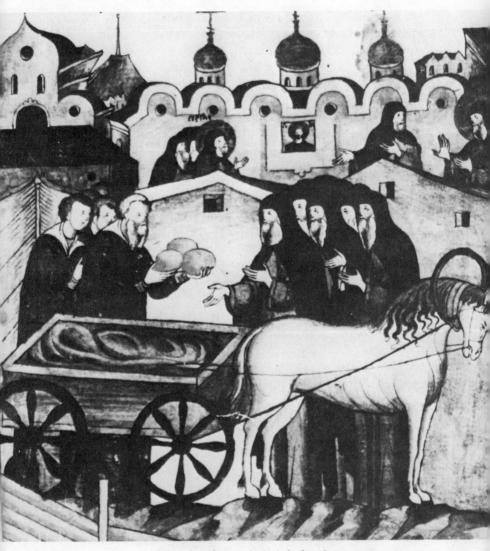

The miraculous arrival of the bread.

arrive. From that day on, there was never any discontent amongst the monks over food, even though they were lacking it from time to time.

The holy abbot never wore a new habit nor "German cloth, colored or white and of good quality, but always ordinary cloth." His habit was old and patched. One day, he found a piece of material that no one would use. He cut it and made a cassock for himself. Visitors to the monastery could not believe that the abbot wore such a poor cassock.

One day, a peasant who had never seen Saint Sergius arrived at the monastery. Saint Sergius was out working in the garden. The visitor asked the monks for "Saint Sergius, this famous and glorious man." The monks told him that the abbot was in the garden. When he saw a poorly dressed man, he refused to believe that it was Saint Sergius. The peasant said to the monks: "I came to see a prophet and you show me a beggar. I came a long way to save my soul and I see that it was all in vain. I had hoped to see Saint Sergius in all his glory and splendor but I see neither splendor nor glory nor beautiful clothes nor servants following him. No, this is not Saint Sergius." Then the monks asked Saint Ser-

gius for permission to expel the peasant, but the abbot said: "This man did not hurt you in any way. He came to see me, only wishing the best for me." Without awaiting a greeting from the peasant, he bowed profoundly before him, kissed him, took him by the hand, sat him down near him and gave him some food. Nevertheless, the peasant was still dissatisfied. "I came to see Saint Sergius, but my desire was not fulfilled." Saint Sergius comforted him and told him that if he trusted in God he would see what he had been looking for. At this time, a richly clothed prince arrived with a great retinue. His servants pushed the peasant away from the saint and from the prince, who, upon seeing the abbot, prostrated himself before him. The saint blessed him and the two sat while everyone else remained standing. The peasant asked one of those near him who the monk was who was sitting next to the prince. The man was surprised and said: "How have you come here without knowing our Father Sergius?" Then the peasant realized his error. He bowed down before Saint Sergius, who raised him up and sent him away in peace. He returned several years later and became a monk in the Trinity Monastery, where he died.

As the number of monks increased, water began to be scarce and it had to be brought from far away. Soon the monks began to complain that Saint Sergius had built his hermitage too far from a sufficient water supply. He said to them: "I wanted to live alone, but God wanted to establish a monastery to the glory of His name." He immediately left the monastery, accompanied by one monk, went down into a little ravine where there was a little water left from the rain, knelt down and prayed. Then he blessed the spot and suddenly a plentiful spring shot up, which supplied water for the monastery up to the present day. Many pilgrims were cured by this water, and people took it to the sick to heal them. They called it Sergius' fountain, but the saint forbade this, saying that God, and not he, had given this water to His unworthy servants.

"There was living in the area of the monastery a man who loved Christ and who had a great devotion to Saint Sergius. His only child became fatally ill. He took him to the lavra

Saint Sergius makes a cassock from cloth rejected by everyone else.

97

The miraculous spring.

and asked the abbot to pray for his recovery. While he was
explaining his case to Saint Sergius, the child died. The an-
guished father cried out: 'It would have been better if the
child had died at home,' and went to find a coffin for his
son. The saint had pity on this man and knelt by the little
body and prayed. All of a sudden, the child came back to
life and the father, who had brought all of the things for the
funeral, received him from Saint Sergius' hands. He thanked
him joyfully, but the saint said, 'You were wrong. The child
was not dead.' The man insisted and said: 'It was by your
prayers that my son was raised from the dead.' Then the
abbot forbade him to speak of this. It was not until much
later that there was an account of this miracle by one of his
disciples.

"A certain lord lived far from the monastery on the banks
of the Volga. He was possessed by a demon; he broke iron
chains and no one could control him. His relatives, having
heard of Saint Sergius, decided to bring him to the Trinity
Monastery, but he fought and refused to enter into this holy
place. Saint Sergius was informed of the arrival of the possessed man. He called together the entire community and
prayed for the healing of the sick man. The possessed man
relaxed and was brought into the monastery, but when Saint

Sergius came to meet him, blessing him with the Holy Cross, he ran away and threw himself into a pond of water, crying: 'What a violent flame!' He was cured by the grace of God and the prayers of the saint, and when they asked him why he threw himself into the pond, he answered, 'I thought that there was a flame coming from the Cross which would devour me.'

"One night while Saint Sergius was praying, he heard a voice calling his name. He was greatly surprised by this and, having finished his prayers, he opened the window to see who had called him. A miraculous vision appeared before him. A great light coming from heaven made the night as bright as day. A second time, a voice called him saying, 'Sergius, you pray for your children and the Lord has heard your prayer. See how many monks have come together in honor of the Holy Trinity to be guided by you.' Then the saint saw a multitude of birds who were not only on the walls of the monastery but also in the clearing surrounding it. The voice said: 'The number of your monks will be as the number of birds, and it will not decrease if they follow your path.' Desiring to have a witness to this vision, Saint Sergius called Archimandrite Simon, but he could only see the light. They rejoiced greatly over this awesome vision."

Healing of the demoniac.

One day, envoys from the Ecumenical Patriarch of Constantinople, Philotheus (1354-76), arrived at the monastery. Bowing before the abbot, they said, "The Ecumenical Patriarch blesses you." They gave him gifts and a letter. Saint Sergius told them that they must be mistaken, but they insisted that they had been sent to him. He immediately went to Moscow and showed the letter to Metropolitan Alexis, who read it. "By the grace of God, Archbishop of Constantinople and Ecumenical Patriarch, Lord Philotheus. May favor, peace and our blessing in the Holy Spirit be with our

The monastery receives envoys from the Patriarch of Constantinople.

son and fellow-server, Sergius. We have heard of your virtuous life in God but you are still lacking the common life. You know that the prophet David could find nothing more praiseworthy than the beauty of brothers dwelling in unity (Ps. 133). This is why we suggest that you introduce the common life, and the grace divine and the blessing of God will be with you."

Saint Sergius asked the Metropolitan: "What do you suggest, my Lord?" Metropolitan Alexis answered: "Because you are worthy of such a divine favor, and because your name and life are known in far-away lands, the Patriarch has given you this advice for the good of all. We are very grateful to the Patriarch." The patriarchal decision was very difficult for Saint Sergius, but he obeyed his superiors. While still abbot, he wanted to remain the servant of all and a teacher rather than an administrator. The rule which was to be introduced in the lavra was rigid and required that he organize life along the lines formerly accepted by Saint Theodosius of Kiev and the other founders of cenobitic monasteries. Saint Sergius obediently accepted the responsibility for organizing the new monastic life. He appointed an economos and an ecclesiarch and distributed the domestic responsibilities among the monks, instructing them to keep the rules of the Church Fathers and to hold all things in common. The number of monks and gifts continued to grow.

TROUBLES IN THE LAVRA AND
THE DEPARTURE OF SAINT SERGIUS

The first difficulties arose because of the difficult and fiery character of Saint Sergius' elder brother, the abbot Stephen, who, having left his monastery in Moscow, had come to live in the Trinity Lavra. By introducing the cenobitic life, the saint had aroused some dissatisfaction among those monks who did not wish to separate from their personal belongings. The reform caused extreme complications for the duties of the superior. It was necessary to build a bakery, a refectory, and pantries. To spiritual direction was added the responsibility of the daily administration of the life of the monastery, which at this time had more

than a hundred monks. The abbot had to direct the offices, and it was in the church, over an insignificant episode, that the split begun by the reform took a drastic turn. Epiphanius does not mention the difficulties which Saint Sergius encountered in the application of this rule, but the events which followed it cannot be explained by the one incident with his brother, no matter how painful it was. From the beginning of the reform, the saint saw that his new life occupied too much of his time and took him too far away from his ideal of a life in silence and humility.

One day, Saint Sergius was in the altar and his brother Stephen in the choir. Stephen asked the canonarch, "Who gave you this book?" The monk answered, "The abbot gave it to me." "Who is the superior?" asked Stephen, "I was the first here," and he went on to say things which he should not have said. The saint did not interrupt, but after the service he did not return to his cell, but left the monastery without anyone seeing him. He returned to the way of the desert, of silence and humility. We do not believe that he did it only because of the words of his brother. Saint Sergius had acquired extraordinary calm and serenity. It seems impossible to think that he spontaneously left that which God had given to him. We do not know the real motives for his departure, but we can suppose that an interior voice guided him to leave his monastery for the good of the monks.

Saint Theodosius of Kiev would have acted differently and would have strictly applied the rule. He would even have chastised those who had broken the rule of total obedience to the abbot. But Saint Sergius wished to give a lesson of humility to those who were still attached to their jobs and their belongings. He left all and went again to seek a place where he could pray to God in solitude. He stopped at the monastery of his friend Abbot Stephen. A former monk of Kiev, he had spent several years in Galicia. In 1349 he left for the monastery of the Trinity, where he had been received by Saint Sergius. After several years of life with the holy abbot, he left the monastery for solitude and founded the hermitage of Makhrishchi, which became another monastery of the Trinity, about 30 kilometers from the Trinity-Saint Sergius Lavra. Saint Sergius asked Abbot Stephen for a monk who could show him to a solitary spot in the area. They visited the neighboring forests and Saint Sergius chose a clearing on the banks of the Kirzhach River, where he built a chapel and a cell. The monks of the Trinity Lavra were distraught over the departure·of their abbot, and some went to look for him in the area. One went to Abbot Stephen and learned from him the place to which the saint had retired. He returned quickly to the monastery and told the news to the monks. Many of them decided to follow their abbot and went to the newly founded monastery on the banks of the Kirzhach. Saint Sergius received them as he had done at the Trinity Lavra, building their cells and organizing the community life. He sent two of his monks to Moscow, to ask Metropolitan Alexis for permission to build a church. This time, he was aided not only by the monks but by numerous volunteers who came to visit him. Princes and boyars came to this new monastery, bringing their gifts. Certain monks who had stayed at the Trinity Monastery were nevertheless very much attached to their abbot and decided to go to Moscow to ask Metropolitan Alexis to order Saint Sergius to return to the Trinity Monastery to re-establish order. The metropolitan sent two archimandrites to Saint Sergius who said to him, "Your father, Metropolitan Alexis, blesses you. He rejoices greatly in hearing of your life in solitude. Now that you have founded a church and a community, you must place at its head one of your disciples and return to the Trinity Lavra so that the monks do not abandon it. Those who refuse to obey you will have to leave the monastery on our order. You must obey us. May the grace of God and our blessing be always with you." The saint answered, "Say to my Lord the metropolitan: 'I accept with joy all that you have said as though Christ Himself had said it to me, and I obey'." The metropolitan ordered the consecration of the new monastery's church in honor of the Annunciation of the Mother of God. Saint Sergius left his disciple Romanus as abbot and returned to his lavra after four years of absence (1358-1362).

He had wanted to leave his disciple Isaac the Quiet as abbot of the Annunciation Monastery, but he categorically

Saint Sergius, having retired to the banks of the Kirzhach, receives the monks who wish to follow him.

refused and asked Saint Sergius to give him a blessing for perpetual silence. Saint Sergius blessed him and said, "May the Lord hear your prayer." At the moment of the blessing, Isaac saw a flame come forth from the saint's hand and surround him completely. He also remained silent until his death, and when he was involuntarily on the point of speaking, he was saved from it by the prayers of Saint Sergius.

The return of Saint Sergius to his lavra was a great feast for those monks who had remained faithful to him.

105

They came out to meet him, kissing his hands, touching the hem of his garment, and giving thanks to God. Those who had provoked his departure had left, and peace was finally restored in the monastery.

THE ESTABLISHMENT OF MONASTERIES

The first monastery which Saint Sergius had founded before he left the Trinity Lavra was the Monastery of the Savior in Moscow. During his journey to Constantinople in 1354, Metropolitan Alexis had undergone a terrible tempest in the Black Sea. He vowed to build a monastery in Moscow, dedicated to the saint of the day upon which they would arrive in a port. The boat entered the Bosporus on August 16, the feast of the icon of the Savior "not made by hands." Upon his return to Russia, the metropolitan asked Saint Sergius to supply an abbot for this monastery, and even suggested the monk Andronicus as the candidate for this position. The saint, who was always obedient to his bishop, allowed his disciple to go to Moscow and establish a monastery. Like Saint Sergius, Andronicus was from Rostov. He was one of the first to come to his hermitage and was one of his most beloved disciples. He was a very humble monk who was always occupied with prayer and the manual labor assigned to him. He left for Moscow and founded a church in honor of the Savior on the banks of the Yauza River. During a second trip to Constantinople, Metropolitan Alexis brought back an ancient icon of Savior "not made by hands" which he placed in this church. Andronicus built cells and organized the monastery, which Saint Sergius often visited. He remained abbot until his death in 1335, when he was succeeded by Sabbas. Both were canonized by the Russian Church. It was under his second successor, Abbot Alexander, that the Church of the Savior was rebuilt and painted with frescoes by two monks of the monastery, the famous iconographer Andrei Rublev and his companion Daniel the Black. The tombs of the two founders of the monastery, as well as those of the two painters, along with some of Rublev's icons from the iconos-tasis, remained until the eve of the Revolution.

Another monastery was also founded in Moscow by Saint Sergius' nephew Theodore, the son of his elder brother Stephen. Theodore was brought to the Trinity Monastery at the age of twelve and remained near the saint, who loved him very much and taught him continually. The young monk never left the saint and lived in a cell very near to his. When he was ordained priest, he decided to found his own monastery. Saint Sergius withheld his blessing for a while, but then permitted him to take several monks from the Trinity Lavra. Theodore found a location which was ex-ceptionally beautiful and not far from the river. Saint Sergius visited the spot and gave his blessing for building a monastery dedicated to the Nativity of the Mother of God. Metropolitan Alexis raised him to the rank of abbot and the Grand Prince Dmitri made him court chaplain. Since there was a road which passed right next to the monastery, Theodore decided to move it closer to the river, where it remained until its destruction after the Revolution. Saint Sergius often came to see his nephew, and they built a special cell for him. The Monastery of the Virgin, com-monly called Simonov after the place where it was built, became one of the richest and most famous monasteries in the area. Many of its monks became abbots of monasteries, and others became bishops. The "Life" of Saint Sergius adds several very important words about his relations with this new monastery and its abbot. "Because of his many virtues, Theodore was venerated by everyone. So much so that Saint Sergius worried and prayed continually that God would save his nephew from all temptation. Here we see how much the humble abbot of the Trinity Lavra worried about the worldly glory which was not befitting a monk." In 1383, Theodore accompanied Bishop Dionysius of Suzdal to Constantinople, where the Ecumenical Patriarch bestowed on him the title of archimandrite and precedence over all the abbots in Russia. He became the first archbishop of Rostov, and ruled his vast diocese with great wisdom for five years (1390-1395). He was a talented iconographer and painted several icons for his monastery in Moscow as well as for the cathedral in Rostov, where he was buried. In speaking of the life of Theodore of Rostov, Epiphanius recounts a miraculous event which took place when the young priest Theodore was celebrating the Liturgy with his uncle. "One day, when Theodore was still living in the monastery, Saint Sergius served the Divine Liturgy with his brother and his nephew. Isaac the Quiet saw near the altar a fourth priest who was glowing with a great light. He then asked the monk Macarius, who was next to him, 'What is this miraculous vision, my father?' The monk Macarius answered him, 'I do not know, but I behold a great and awesome vision.' After the Liturgy, the two monks asked Saint Sergius what

Theodore is brought to the monastery; later he receives a blessing to go to Moscow to found a monastery there.

it had been. Not wishing to reveal what had happened, he said, 'What did you see that was miraculous, my children? There were no other priests besides my brother and my nephew.' The disciples persisted in asking him to tell them what it was. Then Saint Sergius answered them, 'If God revealed it to you, I do not wish to hide it. That which you saw was an angel of the Lord, with whom I, although unworthy, always serve. But do not say anything about what you saw as long as I am alive.' And the disciples were astonished."

The third monastery founded by Saint Sergius was that of Our Lady on the Mountain, on the banks of the Nara River. In 1374, Prince Vladimir of Serpukhov asked the saint to establish a monastery. Saint Sergius chose the location of the future monastery and sent the monk Athanasius, who had been one of his first companions. A learned priest who worked with manuscripts, Athanasius remained abbot of the new monastery until 1401, when he left for Constantinople. He became a monk at the monastery of Saint Theodore the Studite, where he dedicated the last years of his life to the translation of patristic and liturgical texts from Greek to Slavonic.

Finally, a fourth monastery was founded by Saint Sergius at Kolomna, at the request of the Grand Prince Dmitri. The holy abbot walked to the city and chose a spot called Golutvine, where he established the Monastery of the Theophany, with Gregory, one of his disciples, as abbot.

SAINT SERGIUS AND THE STATE

The two "Lives" of Saint Sergius are very quiet about anything concerning the national role of the saint and his part as a peacemaker in the affairs of the principalities. They speak clearly of the blessing given to the Grand Prince Dmitri for his fight against the Mongols, but omit the episode of the mission of the two monks. It is thus necessary to turn to chronicles to bring out certain important facts.

In 1358, the saint returned to Rostov and persuaded Prince Constantine to recognize the authority of Grand

Prince John II. In 1363, he renewed his efforts in order to keep this prince from raising an army against Moscow and starting another fratricidal war. Finally, in 1365, he was sent by Metropolitan Alexis to Nizhni-Novgorod to convince Prince Boris of Suzdal to withdraw his troops from the city, which he had illegally occupied. It was the only time that Saint Sergius, on the order of the metropolitan, had recourse to severe measures. He closed the churches of Nizhni-Novgorod, something which had never been done before. Grand Prince Dmitri also sent him on a peace mission to Prince Oleg of Riazan. Saint Sergius carried out these missions through obedience to the metropolitan, who was the regent of the state.

In 1380, when the Tartar Khan Mamai led a new invasion of Russia, the situation was totally different. The Mongol khans protected the principality of Tver, and feared the growing power of Moscow. They led expeditions against the cities and principalities which aided Moscow. One of their chiefs sacked Nizhni-Novgorod in 1377, and Murza Begich set out against Moscow. The Grand Prince met and fought him on the banks of the Vozha River. It was necessary to prepare for war. This was the first time since the great invasion of 1238-1240 that the Russians dared to confront the Mongol Horde. Khan Mamai assembled a large army and decided to advance against Moscow. He made an alliance with the Grand Prince of Lithuania and camped on the Don, at the mouth of the Voronezh River. At this time, there was no vision among the Russian princes, and it was only through great effort that the Grand Prince was able to assemble an army which could resist the Mongols. Since Metropolitan Alexis had died in 1378, there was no longer a metropolitan in Russia, and the only person to whom he could turn for advice was the holy abbot of the Trinity Monastery. The Grand Prince, accompanied by several princes and military leaders, came to the monastery and asked Saint Sergius if he should confront the enemy. The humble monk held in his hands the future of the country. When Prince Dmitri arrived at the monastery on August 18, 1380, Saint Sergius said to him, "My Lord, your duty requires that you defend your people. Be prepared to offer your soul and spill your blood. But first, go to the khan as his vassal and try to stop him through your submission by explaining the truth to him. The Holy Scripture teaches us that if our enemies want our glory, or if they desire our gold and silver, we can give it to them. Let us only offer our life for the Faith in the name of Christ. Give them your glory and riches, and God will not permit your defeat. Seeing your humility He will exalt you and will humble their great pride." The Grand Prince answered that all attempts at avoiding war had been tried but had been in vain. The saint answered, "Then they will perish. God will come to your aid. May his grace be with you." The holy abbot gave the prince two monks to accompany him, Alexander Peresviet, a former boyar from Briansk, and Irodion Osliabia, a former boyar of Lybut, both experienced warriors.

The next day the Grand Prince set out, and arrived at Kolomna on August 20. Fifteen miles from Moscow he had a vision of Saint Nicholas, who blessed him. On August 27 he crossed the Oka and approached the Don. He stayed there several days, waiting for the Mongol army. Considering the importance and the caliber of the Tartar troops, with whom were united the Lithuanian warriors and those of Oleg of Riazan, the leaders counselled the prince to be prudent. But he, strengthened by Saint Sergius' blessing, crossed the Don and stopped on the bank of the Nepriadva River, in a vast plain called the "Field of Woodcocks" (Kulikovo Pole). The holy abbot had sent him the following message, "Advance without fear, my Lord. Dare to meet their ferocity, and do not fear, for God will assist you." The September 8, 1380, remains a memorable date for Russia. The army rose before the dawn. The soldiers prayed and prepared to die. The combat was clearly unfair. The Tartars appeared around noon. The Grand Prince advanced at the head of his warriors before the first attack. Legend holds that a Tartar soldier provoked the Russians and that one of the monks sent by Saint Sergius went out to meet him and fell, slain. The battle-front extended for more than ten miles. Saint Sergius, who had predicted to Prince Dmitri that the martyr's crown awaited most of the warriors, was not wrong. The battle was bloody and terrible. The Mongols penetrated the Russians' front line and

The Battle of Kulikovo.

the retreat began. Then Prince Vladimir of Serpukhov and the boyar Bobrok, who had been waiting in ambush, attacked the Tartars' flank and began the defeat. During the time of the battle, Saint Sergius was praying to God with

112

the monks in church. He knew everything that was happening and named each one who had died, praying for their souls. Towards the end, he announced to the community that the Russians had won. The Grand Prince returned to Moscow by way of the monastery when they were serving a *molieben* (a service of thanksgiving). On the advice of Saint Sergius, the Grand Prince decided to dedicate the first Saturday after the Feast of Saint Demetrius of Thessalonica to the memory of soldiers who fell to defend Christianity and the country. In keeping with his vows, he built two monasteries. One in Dubenka, on a spot chosen by Saint Sergius, was dedicated to the Dormition of the Mother of God. The other was built on the spot where he had the vision of Saint Nicholas. This monastery, known as the Saint Nicholas Ugreshsky Lavra, had a wonderworking icon of Saint Nicholas of Myra.

The great victory at the field of Kulikovo did not put an end to the Mongol invasions. Wishing to avenge Mamai's defeat, the Khan Tokhtamysh attacked Russia. Unable to resist him, the Grand Prince withdrew to the north, and Saint Sergius and his monks had to leave their monastery for a while. Moscow was sacked, but the Mongols did not reach the monastery, which remained intact.

In 1385, the Grand Prince asked the saint to go to see Oleg of Riazan, an ally of the Tartars at the time of the battle of Kulikovo, and a fierce enemy of Moscow. Despite his age, Saint Sergius set out on foot for Riazan, which was more than 200 kilometers from his monastery. As the chronicles states, "Speaking gently and tenderly, the wonderworking abbot spoke with the prince about the soul, peace and charity, and changing his ferocity into gentleness, the prince calmed down and his soul became tender. Before such a holy man, he was ashamed of his deeds, and with his friendship, he promised the Grand Prince peace for all the generations to come." This was the last intervention by Saint Sergius in state affairs. If he used his moral authority to bring peace to the country, he never allowed secular or ecclesiastical powers to use this power for their own benefit. No one could force the holy hermit to act against his convictions, or to follow a way different from that to which he had been called by Christ.

SAINT SERGIUS AND THE HIERARCHY

We have seen how obedient Saint Sergius was to his chief hierarch, Metropolitan Alexis. Before establishing his hermitage, he had asked Metropolitan Theognostus' blessing. When Bishop Athanasius ordered him to accept the position of abbot, he submitted himself to his will. Each time that Metropolitan Alexis had charged him with a mission, he faithfully carried it out. But when he wanted him to carry out a mission which he considered as contrary to his vocation, he categorically refused it.

In 1378, the Russian Church was in a state of turmoil. When the old Metropolitan Alexis realized his illness, he decided to find a successor who could carry on his work. He belonged to the high nobility of Chernigov. His father had been a governor of Moscow and a collaborator with Prince Daniel. He had received a brilliant education but had chosen the monastic life and spent several years in the same monastery where Stephen, the elder brother of Saint Sergius, lived. Vicar-General of Moscow and then Bishop of Vladimir, he had been sent to Constantinople and in 1354 was consecrated Metropolitan of all Russia by the Patriarch. He was a true prince of the Church, an able diplomat and an accomplished statesman. He had become regent of the state at the time of Grand Prince Dmitri. Metropolitan Alexis had made several trips into the Mongol Horde, cured the wife of Khan Taidula of blindness, and received exemptions and privileges for the Church. He respected Saint Sergius and wanted him as his successor. Grand Prince Dmitri was inclined to support Archimandrite Michael, who, according to the Metropolitan, was too inexperienced for such an important position. On the other hand, the Grand Duke of Lithuania had asked the Patriarch of Constantinople to consecrate a metropolitan for the western provinces, and he had named Bishop Cyprian to this position. When Saint Sergius was called to Moscow by Metropolitan Alexis, he ordered a golden pectoral cross, studded with precious jewels, to be brought to him and wished to place it on the abbot's neck. Saint Sergius said, "Pardon me, father, but from my youth I have not liked gold, and I wish to remain poor in my old age." The metropolitan answered him, "I know this well, but obey me and take what I give you. Do you know why I called you? I wish to find someone who can shepherd the Lord's flock after my death. You alone are worthy of this. I am sure that everyone, from the princes to the poorest peasants, wishes to have you as a shepherd. Therefore, you will be ordained bishop, and you

Metropolitan Alexis wishes to choose Saint Sergius as his successor.

will be my successor after my death." When the saint heard these words, he was greatly troubled because he felt that he was unworthy of this task. "What you propose to me is beyond my abilities. You will not find what you are looking for in me. I am only a sinner and least among men." Metropolitan Alexis tried to convince him but it was in vain.

Saint Sergius refused categorically and said, "Say nothing more if you do not want my poverty to be alienated from your holiness," and he returned to his monastery.

Sometime later a Greek bishop from Constantinople came from Moscow. He had heard of Saint Sergius but did not want to believe that there were saints in Russia. "How could such men live in this country?" He then decided to go to the Trinity Monastery. When he approached the monastery and saw Saint Sergius from a distance, he was seized with fear and lost his sight. The saint took him by the hand and led him into his cell. The bishop then asked him to cure him of this blindness with which he had been stricken for his lack of faith. The saint touched his eyes, and they were opened. Then he said to the bishop, "My most honorable Lord, you must teach us and not exalt yourself in your pride above us. You wished to test us, but that is not good for anyone." Then the bishop said, "Thanks be to God that he let me see a truly heavenly man and an angel." The saint led him away with all due honor, and he returned to his country.

MIRACLES AND VISIONS

Not far from the monastery there lived a man who became fatally ill and lived for twenty days without eating or sleeping. His brothers brought him to the monastery and set him at the saint's feet, asking him to pray for his cure. Saint Sergius prayed and sprinkled him with holy water. He immediately felt relieved and sometime later, completely cured, was able to return home alone. One day, Prince Vladimir, who greatly venerated Saint Sergius, sent him some gifts. The man carrying them stole part of them. When he arrived at the monastery and wished to give them to the abbot, Saint Sergius asked him why he had stolen some of them. The man fell on his knees and asked pardon for his misdeed. Saint Sergius asked him to never do it again and then forgave him.

The "Life" reports another incident which shows us how Saint Sergius chastised those who had committed an injustice. One of the rich landowners in the area had stolen a pig from one of his poor neighbors who could not defend himself. The latter went to seek protection and justice from Saint Sergius, who called the rich man and, having admonished him, told him to pay the price of the pig and return it to the poor man. He agreed, but then changed his mind and decided to pay nothing. He then ordered that the pig be killed and put in his cellar, but the next day, in spite of the bitter cold, he found that it had been eaten by maggots. Then, seeing in this his just punishment, he went to his poor neighbor and paid him everything that he owed him.

On another occasion, Saint Sergius was celebrating the Divine Liturgy in the presence of his disciple Simon the Ecclesiarch. Simon had an extraordinary vision. He said that during the Liturgy, he saw a fire which touched the table of prothesis and surrounded the holy altar. At the moment of communion, the fire entered the chalice and the saint received communion in this manner. Seeing this, Simon was filled with terror and fear. The saint understood that Simon had had an extraordinary vision and said to him, "My son, why are you terrified?" He answered, "Master, I never had an awesome vision. I saw the grace of the Holy Spirit acting with you." Then the saint forbade him to speak of it. "Do not tell anyone what you saw until I die."

VISIT OF THE ALL-HOLY MOTHER OF GOD

One of the characteristic traits of Saint Sergius' life is that no women were ever involved in it. He had no carnal temptations in his youth, and throughout his life no nun or female relative ever came to see him. He never founded a convent as did Saint Seraphim. It has been said that he was not concerned with female piety. This is the impression which we receive from the accounts of his contemporaries. Nevertheless, the veneration of the Mother of God was central in Saint Sergius' life. Every night he sang

hymns in honor of the Theotokos, and at the end of his life, he had the privilege of a visit. The "Life" states that our all-venerable father was praying before the icon of the all-pure Mother of our Lord Jesus Christ. Looking at the icon, he said, "Most pure Mother of my Christ, powerful protectress of men, be our protectress and pray to your son and our God that he will keep this place consecrated to the glory of His name for all eternity." Thus he prayed and sang the praises of the Virgin. Having finished his prayer, he sat down to rest a bit and said to his disciple Mica, "Stay awake, my son, for we will have a miraculous visit." As soon as he had said these words, a voice proclaimed, "The all-holy is coming." The saint heard this call and arose and went to the door of his cell. A light brighter than the sun illumined it, and he saw the all-holy, surrounded by an ineffable light, with the two apostles, Peter and John, by her side. When the saint saw them, he fell to the ground because he could not bear the overly powerful light. The all-holy touched his hand and said to him, "Do not be afraid, my chosen one. I have come to visit you. Your prayer for your disciples and your monastery has been heard. Worry no more. Henceforth, your monastery will lack nothing, not only during your life, but after your death and your return to God. I will ceaselessly protect this place and watch over it." After she said this, she left him. The saint was seized with a great fear and ecstasy. Arising, he saw his disciple Mica prostrated and he lifted him up. Mica threw himself at the old man's feet and asked him, "Tell me what this miraculous vision was, for my soul was ready to leave my body because of this brilliant light." The saint was rejoicing in his spirit and his face shone with joy, but he could not say anything to him. He said simply, "Be patient, my son, for my spirit trembles before this vision." Thus they remained without talking for a while. Then the saint said to his disciple, "My son, call Isaiah and Simon," and when they entered, he told them all that had taken place. They listened and were filled with a great joy. All four began to pray, and they sang a service in honor of the Mother of God and glorified the Creator. The saint spent

The descent of fire upon the altar.

119

the entire night without sleeping, meditating on the miraculous apparition.

THE DEATH OF SAINT SERGIUS

Saint Sergius had spent many years in prayer, fasting and work. Although he was very old, he never missed any of the services. As he grew older, he became more ardent. Six months before his death, which he had foreseen, he called together all of the monks and entrusted the leadership of the monastery to the oldest and closest of his disciples, Nikon, who was very virtuous. He told him to

Saint Sergius entrusts Saint Nikon with direction of the monastery.

lead Christ's flock with care and justice, and vowed himself to silence. As his death drew nearer, he called everyone together and exhorted them to remain true to Orthodoxy, keeping peace among themselves, purity of body and soul, charity, and avoiding any pollution. He instructed them to avoid the abuse of food and drink and urged them to cultivate humility and hospitality, not seeking earthly glory but awaiting their just rewards from God. He finished with these words: "At the call of God I am leaving you. I entrust you to the almighty Lord. May His most pure mother be a refuge and defense against the snares of the enemy." Supported by his disciples, he received Holy Communion, raised his hands towards heaven, and after a prayer entrusted his holy and pure soul to God, on September 25, 1392. He was 78 years old. His body gave off a sweet fragrance.

Before his death, Saint Sergius had asked to be buried among the monks in the monastery cemetery, but by the order of Metropolitan Cyprian, he was buried under the Church of the Trinity which he had built. Many miracles took place at his tomb: paralytics were cured, those possessed were freed of their evils and the blind regained their sight. Thirty years after his death, his miraculously preserved body was recovered and placed in the church. One day, a pious man of the area had a dream in which the saint told him to tell the abbot that his body was surrounded by water. The man went immediately to abbot Nikon and recounted this dream. They searched beneath the church and found the coffin surrounded by water. When they opened it, they all saw that the saint's body and clothes had remained intact. The body was placed in a new coffin and put in the newly built church, where it remains until today. An enormous crowd of pilgrims was present for this transfer of the relics on July 5, 1422.

Saint Sergius' work was carried on after his death. Many of his disciples and friends founded monasteries throughout Russia. He was truly the renewer of monasticism in Russia. He was the educator and spiritual guide of the people. For centuries, the lavra carried out this great moral influence on the country.

His example is still living. After World War II, the

The death of Saint Sergius.

great center of prayer which he founded was re-opened. All of the great Russian spiritual movements since the fourteenth century are somehow related to him. We can conclude this account with what Father Rouet de Journel says in his book on Russian monasticism: "He is the most famous and most venerated of all the holy monks. In him, Russia saw the harmonious unity of the inclinations to the eremitical life and to the cenobitic life. It also saw in him the union of contemplative prayer and action, in the sense in which Eastern monks have always understood it: that work which exhausts the body and makes it the servant of the soul, which not only produces food for the worker but also allows him to share it with others, that work which is humility, self-denial and charity. Russia revered Sergius as the founder of a monastery in which poverty and obedience reigned in an atmosphere of fervor."

THE DISCIPLES AND FRIENDS OF SAINT SERGIUS

First among Saint Sergius' disciples was Saint Nikon, his successor as abbot of the Trinity Lavra. He was from the city of Yuriev-in-the-Fields (Polsky), which is half way between Rostov and Radonezh. At a very early age, he came to the monastery, where Saint Sergius put him under the guidance of his disciple, Athanasius. When Athanasius was sent by Saint Sergius to establish the monastery of the Theotokos on the Mountain, Nikon went with him. Having returned in 1375 to the Trinity Lavra, he became the saint's closest co-worker. During the last years of Saint Sergius' life, he even lived in the same cell with him. He was abbot of the Trinity Lavra from 1392 until his death in 1426. He rebuilt the entire lavra, which had been destroyed during the invasion by Khan Tokhtamysh in 1408. In 1412, after the discovery of Saint Sergius' relics, he commissioned the famous iconographer Andrei Rublev to paint an icon of the Holy Trinity. He had him and Daniel the Black paint the iconostasis (1422-26). He also accepted the first land gifts to the monastery from the princes. These lands were

Saint Nikon has the new church decorated by Rublev.

very important and brought great revenues to the monastery. The profits enabled Saint Nikon to build a cathedral and to relieve much misery, but the monastery was no longer able to live in the great poverty which its founder had bequeathed it. Saint Nikon, who was not only a great administrator but also a monk and an exemplary ascetic, was canonized by the Russian church in 1547.

The Church of the Holy Trinity which Saint Nikon had built, held Saint Sergius' wooden chalice, his simple cloth vestments and the two icons which he had in his cell. The servant of the Trinity, who had always been "like unto

124

Christ" had a special devotion to the Theotokos and to Saint Nicholas. He always had in his cell an icon of the Theotokos: "Umilenie" (tenderness, compassion), and an icon of Saint Nicholas, the patron saint of Russia.

Let us look at seven more of Saint Sergius' disciples, who were builders of monasteries and continuers of the work of their spiritual master.

From his youth, Saint Sabbas (Savva) was a "very obedient" disciple of Saint Sergius. He became the confessor of the community and many monks came to the monastery to seek guidance from him. Saint Sergius sent him to be abbot of the Dubensky monastery, but he returned several times to the Trinity-Saint Sergius Lavra dur-

The iconostasis painted by Rublev.

ing Abbot Nikon's absences. Nikon could go on a long, solitary retreat in order to gain strength for guiding the monastery. At the request of the monks, Sabbas would come to replace him. At the request of the prince of Zvenigorod, in 1398 he established a monastery dedicated to the Nativity of the Theotokos, which he led until his death in 1407. Saint Sabbas was particularly venerated by Tsar Alexis, who donated heavily to his monastery.

Saint Methodius of Peshnosh worked at the Trinity Lavra under the direction of Saint Sergius, who gave him permission to leave the monastery in order to lead the eremitical life. He spent several years in the forests. In 1361, after several monks had joined him, he began a monastery on the Peshnosh River. The poverty of this place was so great that when Methodius celebrated the Liturgy, he used a wooden chalice. Following Saint Sergius' example, he built the church and cells.

Saint Sergius of Nurom, who built a monastery on the river of the same name, was also a hermit and a great ascetic. He spent many years in solitude in the depths of the forests of the Vologda region. He died in 1412.

Saint Sylvester of Obnosk, a beloved student of Saint Sergius, founded the monastery of the Resurrection in the area of Yaroslavl (1379). His monastery, like those of Saint Sabbas and Saint Sergius of Nurom, was closed in 1764 under Catherine II.

Monks often left their monasteries with the abbot's permission to go to spend some time with Saint Sergius, in order to receive instruction in the spiritual life from him. Paul (Komelsky) from Moscow was such a monk. He had left the world for the monastery of the Nativity at the age of 22, but had decided to complete this ascetical preparation at the Trinity Lavra. After several years of preparation, Saint Sergius allowed him to leave his monastery. Saint Paul spent fifteen years in total solitude, leading a strict life. He was the most severe ascetic of his time. At the age of 72, he founded a monastery, to which he gave a strict rule, but appointed his disciple Alexander as abbot. He visited the monastery every Sunday. He died in 1429 at the age of 112.

The church of the Trinity Monastery.

Some of Saint Sergius' disciples not only built monasteries but also worked for the transformation of life according to the spirit of Christ. Saint James of the Iron Forest (Zheleznoborovsky) built a chapel and a cell in the northern forests. His monastery was destroyed by the Tartars, but he rebuilt it. His monastery was a center that attracted the neighboring population. Everyone came to him for advice. He taught the young, fed the hungry and sick. During the famine of 1442, he distributed food to the entire starving populace. His grave became a place of pilgrimage where more than fifty cures were reported among those who came to ask his help.

Finally, Saint Abraham of Galich, a monk vowed to total silence, established four monasteries around Lake Chukhloma. These monasteries were cultural centers for the entire area. They were closed by Catherine II at the time of the secularization (1764).

Saint Sergius' disciples founded almost thirty monasteries and were instrumental in spreading the word of God, even though they were not missionaries in the technical sense of the word. The forests where they built their hermitages were uninhabited. Going further north, the Russians encountered people who were still pagans. Saint Stephen of Perm, the greatest missionary of the Russian Church, was the apostle of this area, which stretched to the Urals and was called "the Great Permia."

Saint Stephen was born in 1340 in the city of Ustiug. His parents, Simeon and Mary, gave him a good education and involved him in church work. He was an exceptionally intelligent and gifted youth. Legend has it that the blessed Procopius of Ustiug predicted to Stephen's mother that her son would be a great servant of God. Stephen was sent to complete his studies in the famous school of Saint Gregory Nazianzen in Rostov. This school had an excellent collection of patristic works, as well as competent instruction in languages. The young man studied Greek and Zirian, the language of a people who lived in his native area. He copied manuscripts and prepared for his work. It was at this time that he became a monk. The presence of many Zirians in Rostov enabled him to translate the Bible and liturgical texts into their language.

Saint Stephen, Bishop of Perm, greets Saint Sergius at a distance.

In 1379, Bishop Gerasimus of Kolomna charged him with the mission of evangelizing the north. For four years, he travelled throughout the area, destroying idols and preaching the Gospel everywhere. He was persecuted several times by some of the people who wanted to kill him. He taught them in their language and converted the entire people. Consecrated as the first bishop of Perm in 1383, he built about ten churches and the monastery of the Archangels. He was not only an apostle but also a father and protector of his adopted people. He defended them against the demands of the central powers, distributed food

129

during the years of scarcity, and helped the poor and old. In 1396, he died while on a trip to Moscow and was buried in the Kremlin.

During one of his trips to Moscow he was in a great rush and could not visit his friend, Saint Sergius. He stopped on the road, which was ten miles from the monastery, and greeted the holy abbot saying: "Rejoice, my brother in the Spirit." Saint Sergius, who was in the refectory at that moment, arose and said before the shocked community: "Rejoice also, pastor of Christ's flock, and may the peace of God be with you." Saint Sergius then told the monks that the Bishop of Perm had bowed before the Holy Trinity and blessed the lavra. In memory of this event, the monks of the Trinity Lavra always rose during the middle of a meal and recited a prayer.

In addition to the monasteries which were established around the Trinity Lavra, there was also the development of a great monastic center in the north at the same time. It was known as the "Russian Thebaid." The White Lake (Beloye Ozero) was the central point around which the eremitical life sprang up in this area.

Pachomius the Logothete, who wrote an abridged version of Saint Sergius' life, also left a life of Saint Cyril of the White Lake. Next to Saint Sergius, he was the most famous and most venerated saint of ancient Russia, but he seems to have been completely forgotten after his time. He was from Moscow and had been for several years the treasurer for his relative, the boyar Veliaminov. He prized Cyril and would not let him leave. No monk in Moscow dared to interfere with this powerful official's wishes. Saint Stephen, on his way to Moscow, received him as a monk. He was admitted to the monastery of the Nativity of the Theotokos (Simonov) in Moscow, where Saint Sergius' nephew Theodore was abbot. Cyril spent several years there, studying with Saint Sergius, who often came to visit his nephew and to speak to the monks. Saint Cyril wished to take on ascetical practices beyond his strength, but his starets controlled his zeal and imposed absolute obedience on him. When Saint Sergius would arrive at the monastery, he would go straight to the bakery where Saint Cyril worked and would spend hours talking to him. Cyril refused to be-

Saint Cyril of the White Lake (15th c.).

come abbot in his monastery. The Holy Virgin appeared to
him in a dream and told him to go to the White Lake. He
took with him the monk Ferapont, who knew the region, and
together they went north. There Cyril founded a monastery
and gave it a very strict cenobitic rule. The monks had no

131

Saint Dmitri Prilutsky.

personal belongings in their cells. All work was done in total silence. The food was always meager, and wine and honey were forbidden. The monastery was extremely poor. Cyril refused any gifts of lands but accepted gifts from nature. Although their poverty did not allow the monks to engage in welfare, Saint Cyril still insisted on active charity. He exhorted the princes to organize their states along Christian lines. He also said that the monk should be the builder of the people. Veneration of the Mother of God and the gift of tears were the two characteristic traits of his piety. Following what would seem to be a law of history, the monastery became one of the largest land owners in northern Russia after Saint Cyril's death. Although its wealth was enormous, its monks still kept the austere rule which their founder had given them.

Ferapont did not stay with Saint Cyril but established a monastery beyond the forest. He was attacked several times by thieves and his neighbors, but each time he rebuilt his little hermitage. He taught many trades to the monks who came to live with him. He refused to become abbot and remained as a simple monk in the monastery. In 1408, on the invitation of the Prince of Mozhaisk, he went to establish a monastery near that city and became its archimandrite. By the end of the fifteenth century his monastery was one of the most important in Russia and equalled that of Saint Cyril. Its frescoes, painted by Master Dionysius, were the most beautiful in Russia.

We end the list of Saint Sergius' friends by mentioning those monks who were known for their hospitality. Saint Dmitri Prilutsky built a monastery dedicated to Saint Nicholas on the banks of Lake Pereslav. He often went to see Saint Sergius, who also visited him. His monastery, as well as the one which he founded in the forests of Vologda, took in the poor and sick and showed a warm hospitality. Saint Euthemius built an urban monastery in the city of Suzdal. He helped the sick and the poor, freed many prisoners, educated the young and protected the weak against the authorities. He often visited Saint Sergius. Saint Euthemius died in 1404 at the age of 88.

The impetus given to the monastic life by Saint Sergius was truly remarkable. From the end of the fourteenth century to the end of the sixteenth century, 150 monasteries were founded in the wilderness and 104 in the cities. Considering the role that these centers of prayer played in the Russian life of their times, it is clear that Saint Sergius was truly the source of a moral influence which, after centuries of Mongol oppression, transformed Russia. The spiritual heritage of Saint Sergius and the influence of his lavra lasted for centuries, and survived the great confusions which later overtook his people and his country.

ПРЕМЫ

The Spiritual Heritage of Saint Sergius

Saint Sergius' influence was not limited to his disciples and friends. It extended over two centuries of Russian monasticism, which can be considered the golden age of Russian spirituality. The period of intense religious life lasted until the end of the seventeenth century. However its center moved to the north and the west. Monasteries were built beyond the polar circle, and persecutions by Ivan the Terrible obliged many churchmen to leave Moscow for Lithuania.

We cannot say that all of the great monasteries founded were in contact with Saint Sergius. Some were his contemporaries, but it is really to the humble abbot of the Trinity Lavra that we must credit this move toward holiness which seized the Russian people after a period of moral depression. As early as the end of the fifteenth century, we see two great spiritual movements clearly moving away from the tradition of Saint Sergius. However their very existence would not have been possible were it not for him.

Saint Paphnutius of Borovsk was the founder of a line of strict ascetics who instigated the movement of the Possessors. Joseph, a monk of Paphnutius' monastery, was the theoretician and undisputed leader of this movement. Another movement, that of the "starets from beyond the Volga," had Saint

Cyril of the White Lake as its spiritual ancestor and Saint Nilus Sorsky as its theoretician. The opposition between these two ideologies, which degenerated into open battle in the sixteenth century and concluded with the victory of the Possessors, shows that these two movements, even though both coming from the same source, were far from the tradi-

The Solovky Monastery, on the White Sea.

tion of Saint Sergius, which alone could preserve a balance in the country's spiritual powers.

Two founders of monasteries, Dionysius Glushitsky and Macarius of Kaliazin, were in a certain way the ancestors of the nineteenth-century startsy, because they received in their monasteries everyone who came to seek their advice. How-

137

ever we will see that, just as with Saint Abraham of Smolensk, the office of starets differed considerably from these prototypes.

A type of saint which was very popular in Russia and which was outside the limits of Saint Sergius' tradition was that of the fools-for-Christ. This type changed drastically in the fifteenth and sixteenth centuries. We have seen that the first fools-for-Christ in Russia were probably German. Those of the era of which we are now speaking were much more humane and their role was clearly more social. They took upon themselves the burden of folly in order to incriminate those who ruled or abused their power. Saint Basil was the "living conscience" of Ivan the Terrible (John IV), who honored him despite his accusations and who personally carried him to his grave in the Church of the Protection of the Theotokos in Moscow's Red Square. The people venerated him so much that the church where he was buried was known as the Church of Saint Basil. Another fool-for-Christ, Nicholas of Novgorod, preached peace between the hostile parties of the commonwealth. These holy ones defended the people against the abuses of power.

In the extreme north, the city of Novgorod the Great was the center of Christian mission and monastic foundations. Although this great city was subjugated by John III of Moscow at the end of the fifteenth century, it still continued its cultural role until the time of Ivan the Terrible, who completely destroyed it in 1570.

The entire north was colonized by Novgorodians in the ninth and tenth centuries. Most of the missionaries going to the Finnish people left from Novgorod. A great center was established in the middle of the fifteenth century on the desert islands of the White Sea. Two monks, Sabbatius and Herman, left for the Solovky Archipelago. Sabbatius returned to the continent a little before his death in 1435, but Herman, who had been joined by another monk, Zosima, decided to establish a monastery on the islands. This monastery soon became one of the most famous and one of the most strict in all of Russia. Not only did it attract monks but also pilgrims, who continued to come until the Revolution in 1917. The monastery of the Transfiguration was not only an exemplary center of monastic life but also a center of civilization. The monks built model farms, workshops and schools on their islands. They had their own navy and received everyone who came to pray or to learn with them. Many young men received a preparation for life there. The two founders of Solovky both died in 1478, but the monastery of Saints Herman and Zosima flourished until 1920. Then the Soviet government turned it into the central prison and place of deportation for clergy and political prisoners. In the seventeenth century, the monastery took part in the Raskol movement and was attacked by government troops. It was occupied by the Swedes several times and in 1855 by the English. The monastery always maintained the same rule which had been introduced by the founders.

Further beyond Solovky, at the extreme border of the Russian lands, was the monastery and cultural center founded by Saint Tryphon of Pechenga. He was born in Novgorod in 1485 and at the call of Christ went to preach the Gospel. In 1532 he built a church on the Norwegian border and established a monastery. Until it was closed by Catherine II, this monastery was a missionary and educational center for all the peoples of the extreme north. The monks built a port, organized fisheries and taught the population to collect birds' down. Restored in 1886, the monastery of Saint Tryphon went to Finland after the Revolution and became a tourist center. The founders of Solovky and Pechenga, who were not disciples of Saint Sergius, had a deep veneration for him and dedicated their churches to him.

If most Russian monks followed the way set out by Saint Sergius, there were still hermits who remained beyond any contact with the world. The most famous of these hermits was Saint Nilus Stolbinsky, who spent 26 years in total silence on a little desert island in Lake Seliger. He had his own garden and very rarely saw fishermen, who banked on his beach from time to time. A great monastery was established after his death on the location of his cell and chapel.

The two great religious movements which divided Russia in the fifteenth century sprang from three fundamental problems of church life: church possessions, relations between Church and state, and the attitude towards heretics. As we have said before, the wealth of the monasteries was rather disturbing. This new situation allowed for social work, but it

Saint Nilus Stolbinsky and his island-monastery.

contradicted the way of poverty and contemplation laid down by Saint Sergius and the monastic founders of the fifteenth century. At the Council of 1504, Grand Prince John III attempted to promulgate a law according to which the state would have the right to take part of the Church's possessions. But the opposition was much stronger and won. It is interesting to note that the head of the opposition, Joseph, Abbot of Volokolamsk, not only fought against the transfer of church goods but also for the independence of the Church from the state. His disciples were the protagonists of an intimate union between the growing autocratic power and the Church. The difference between Joseph's and his opponent Nilus Sorsky's attitudes toward church properties has been greatly exaggerated. Their real opposition was elsewhere. Constantinople had fallen to the Muslims in 1453 and Moscow considered itself as the spiritual heir of Byzantium, giving rise to the theory of Moscow as the Third Rome. Both parties agreed that Russia had to take upon herself the great heritage of the Eastern Empire. But while one group saw it as a holy duty, the other became more and more locked into a nationalism limited to Moscow.

These differing attitudes toward the state reflected differing approaches to the world. The two movements crystallized particularly in their attitudes toward heresy at the end of the fifteenth century.

The rationalist movement, which sprang up in Novgorod in 1471 and which soon took on great proportions, was commonly called the "judaizing heresy." Its origin is still rather mysterious. Perhaps it was influenced by the Hussite movement, but its connections with Arab-Jewish philosophy are much clearer. The books of Maimonides, Averroës and Emmanuel Ben Jacob were among the Judaizers' most precious texts. These heretics were deists who denied the Trinity, the Church, the sacraments and the recognition of any hierarchy. Although condemned by the Council of 1490, they continued their activities until 1504 and were rather solidly implanted in Moscow in the Grand Prince's entourage, attracting many clerical sympathizers. It was over the methods of struggling against the Judaizers that the two monastic currents in Russia were divided. Joseph of Volokolamsk, with his friend Gennadius, Archbishop of Novgorod, called for an intense

141

struggle against the heretics, while Nilus Sorsky preached mercy. Besides these two problems exterior to the spiritual life, the two movements were opposed on the very basis of their spiritual method. Joseph of Volokolamsk (1439-1515), who came from a noble and wealthy family, the Sanins, was a great ascetic and monastic reformer. He established a model monastery and wrote many ascetical and polemical works collected under the title *The Educator*. His monastic rule was based on scripture and tradition, but the liturgical and ritual element played a very great role in it. He could see no necessity for Biblical criticism when the tradition of the Church could take its place.

Nilus Sorsky (1433-1508) also belonged to a wealthy noble family, the Maikovs. He was not formed by Russian monasticism, for he had left early for Mount Athos, where he was influenced by contemporary Greek spirituality and hesychast ideas. When he returned to Russia, he established a skete (a little hermitage), patterned on the sketes of the Holy Mountain. Although his rule was very strict, it was totally different from that of Saint Theodosius and of Saint Sergius. The monks could never live in groups larger than three, and kept their independence in their contemplative life. The rule was based entirely on the New Testament, and Saint Nilus required a serious study of the text. According to him, the only goal of the monastic life was to obtain for man a total freedom, liberated from all earthly cares. If the two spiritual rules deviate from the Russian monastic tradition, the one by its rigidity and intolerance and the other by its absolute negation of the world, nevertheless they are both within the boundaries of Orthodox spirituality, of which they form the two extremes.

Russian monasticism, like Russian spirituality of this period, was not limited to these two large movements. It is necessary to mention the great Orthodox humanist, Maximus the Greek, as well as the immediate heirs of Joseph and Nilus, the monks Philotheus and Vassian. Maximus the Greek was one of the most erudite men of his period. Born of a Greek family, he studied at Corfu under the direction of the Greek scholars John Moschos and John Lascaris, and with the latter he went to Florence and continued his studies in Padua, Bologna, and Venice. He had as teachers Marsilio

Maximus the Greek (Moscow School, ca. 1600).

Ficino, Scipio Callerges, and Fonteguerri. In Florence he became acquainted with Savanarola and gathered his ashes in 1498. He left the Dominican monastery of Saint Mark in 1504 and went to Mount Athos. From then on he was an ardent defender of Orthodoxy. In 1518 at the invitation of Grand Prince Basil III, he arrived in Moscow and headed the movement of religious reform. He published patristic and liturgical translations and his influence stretched over two centuries. Even his ideological adversaries acknowledged his authority and knowledge, but that did not protect him from prosecution. He was sent to a monastery and remained

143

there under house arrest until Abbot Arthemius of Saint Sergius' monastery took him home in 1531.

Russian spirituality was alive in the northern monasteries but in the capital it was becoming more and more obscured by national problems. In 1552, when Metropolitan Daniel, a disciple of Joseph of Volokolamsk, succeeded Metropolitan Joseph, a disciple of Nilus Sorsky, an open struggle began against Maximus the Greek, Vassian and his disciples. The sketes beyond the Volga were closed, and the nationalist tendency definitely took the upper hand over the contemplatives. The idea of Russia as a "Third Rome," the protector of Eastern Christians, degenerated very quickly into Moscow, the "Third Rome," which was the only one to profess Orthodoxy and which considered all other people to be tainted with heresy. This religious ideology provided a religious basis for Basil III's absolutism, which broke with the historical tradition of princely power.

DECLINE AND RENEWAL

After the "time of troubles," Russian spiritual life improved little by little, but the tragedy of internal schism had irreparable effects. The "Raskol" took away the Church's most stable and most traditional elements. It was rooted in the era which we have just studied. The Old Believers continually referred to Maximus the Greek, but they fought against Greek and Western influences. The tragedy of the Raskol was that the most traditional party left the official Church and, while preserving the integrity of the faith, became a separate and persecuted organism which nonetheless grew continually. We cannot stop at this tragedy but we must state that at the moment when Peter the Great began his struggle against the Church, it was so weakened by the strain of the Raskol that it could not react and ceded to the assault of secularization. The eighteenth century was deadly for Russian spirituality. The only spiritual guides were a few bishops who tried to save "Holy Russia."

After a period of intense anti-religious propaganda, with burlesque processions and "false councils," Peter the Great

Peter the Great.

attacked the very basis of the Church and Russian spirituality. Many of the monasteries were closed. Others were turned into insane asylums and hospitals. The patriarchate was abolished and the church government was nominally handed to a college of bishops, but in reality to a procurator-general, who, according to the imperial decree, had to be a "good and bold officer who could control the affairs of the Synod." Consequently, among the procurators-general there were men indifferent to religion and even atheists. Peter himself was a believer. He often sang and read the Hours in church. An icon of Saint Sergius accompanied him everywhere. But having erased the very idea of the Church from his legislation, he had instituted a "spiritual college" which directed the spiritual life of citizens in the same way as cabinet ministers

Catherine II.

145

managed their material life. But Peter the Great did not dare to suppress all the spiritual "foci" in Russia. Many continued to exist, and the Church began a passive struggle against the state for the soul of the Russian people. It was Cathèrine the Great, under the influence of the French Encyclopaedists, who decided to strike the decisive blow against the Church. All of the monasteries were closed in 1746, and their possessions were confiscated by the state. A few were re-opened, but they were totally nationalized. The monasteries were ranked in several classes and received minimal endowments from the state. From the spiritual point of view, the results of Peter the Great's religious reforms were disastrous. The members of the clergy were transformed into bureaucrats and supervisors of the people's good conduct. Catherine II's reform deprived Russia of its most vital sources. Peter the Great had forbidden the acceptance of any new monks, but Elizabeth I had suppressed this law. Catherine II strictly limited the number of those who could enter the contemplative life.

The renewal of the monastic life came from outside. Paissy Velichkovsky (1722-1794), a monk of southern Russia who recognized the impossibility of establishing a spiritual center in Russia, went to Mount Athos and then to Moldavia, where he became abbot of the famous Lavra of Neamt. It was from this monastery that renewers of monasticism spread throughout Russia at the beginning of the nineteenth century. Father Paissy translated patristic works and especially the famous collection known as *The Philokalia* ("Love of Spiritual Beauty") into Slavonic. *The Philokalia* was compiled by Nicodemus, a monk of Mount Athos, and was printed in Greek in Venice in 1772. Abbot Nicodemus was recently canonized by the Greek Church.

We must mention the names of two missionary saints who in the eighteenth century attempted to check the disastrous consequences of secularization and nationalization of the Church. At the beginning of the century, Saint Dmitri (Tuptalo), Metropolitan of Rostov (1651-1709), collected and published the lives of saints and wrote books of spirituality and instruction for the faithful. In the middle of the century, Saint Tikhon (Sokolov), Bishop of Voronezh (1724-83), set out to raise the spiritual level of the clergy and

St. Tikhon of Zadonsk.

monks but soon returned to a monastery in Zadonsk, where
he spent the last fifteen years of his life. His ascetical works
made him one of the most famous spiritual masters of the
Russian Church.

Spiritual renewal in Russia began in 1825, when Saint
Seraphim of Sarov opened the door of his cell and inaugurated the era of the "starets." Two meanings of this word

147

Optino in the 19th c.

are often confused. In a general sense, it means any elderly monk who is charged with the preparation of young novices. There were "startsy" ("old" or "venerable") in all the monasteries from the earliest times. The Russian startsy of the nineteenth century formed a special category in Orthodox spirituality. We have seen that certain monks, such as Saint Abraham of Smolensk, received visitors and gave spiritual guidance to laymen. But the work of Saint Seraphim of Sarov and the nineteenth-century startsy was much greater. The guidance of souls, as Saint John Chrysostom understood it, was their main goal. Their ascetical preparation was aimed at letting others share in their spiritual experience. Saint Seraphim of Sarov (1759-1833), like Saint Theodosius of Kiev, was from the city of Kursk in central Russia. After a life of intense asceticism and prayer, he began to receive those who needed his advice. There was a continuous stream of pilgrims who drew on the spiritual experience of Saint Seraphim. He was the real spiritual master of nineteenth-century Russia. The account of his conversations with Motovilov is the most profound expression of Russian spirituality.

The foundation of another center of startsy was almost parallel to the era of Saint Seraphim. It was the Optino monastery in Kaluga. The difference between the spiritual centers of Sarov and Optino was in the principle of "succession." Saint Seraphim left no spiritual heir, while the startsy of Optino transmitted their spiritual guidance to a successor, who alone bore the title of "starets." Saint Seraphim was visited by everyone from Alexander I to the most humble peasants. The Optino startsy, who belonged to different social classes, were "specialized" in their work as spiritual fathers.

These two centers responded to the deepest aspirations of the Russian people. If Saint Seraphim, whose holiness was recognized even before he began his work as a starets, was not bothered by the ecclesiastical authorities, such was not the case with the first Optino startsy. They were persecuted and were prohibited for having dared to introduce "novelties" into the monastic life. It was by the intervention of the Bishop of Kaluga, Philaret (Amphitheatrov), future Metropolitan of Kiev and himself a great ascetic, that the startsy became an institution accepted by the Church. Leonid, the first of the great Optino startsy, had been a wandering merchant. He had travelled throughout all of Russia and became a monk rather late. Simple and a bit rough, he preferred to counsel simple folk, and used a highly symbolic language. He was starets from 1829 to 1841. His successor, Macarius, was totally different. He was a scholar who loved the arts and philosophy. He worked especially closely with intellectuals. His charitable work was far-reaching and Optino became a spiritual center to which came not only common people but also writers and professors. Macarius, who died in 1860, was succeeded by Ambrose (Amvrossy). Starets Ambrose preferred to speak with the people. Nevertheless, it was during the years 1860-1891, when he was the most famous spiritual guide in Russia, that the Optino monastery attracted the largest audience from all classes of the population. He was followed by

Nesterov's "The Monks" (1862).

Anatolius, Barsanuphius, Joseph, and Nectarius, who was present in 1923 when the Communists closed the monastery. The last Optino starets died in 1928 in a little village in central Russia.

The last quarter of the nineteenth century saw the re-opening of some monasteries. Many new ones were founded after 1880. Two spiritual masters illumined the Russian Church with their ascetical works, Ignatius (Brianchaninov), Bishop of Stavropol (1807-67), and Theophanes (Govorov) "the Hermit," Bishop of Vladimir (1815-94).

At the end of the nineteenth century and the beginning of the twentieth, Father John of Kronstadt (1829-1908) began a profound liturgical movement. His spiritual mission extended throughout Russia and his book, *My Life in Christ*, is still one of the most read of spiritual works.

Finally, a rather limited spiritual movement crystallized around the Jesus Prayer. It was centered in the Russian monastery on Mount Athos and in the Valaam monastery on Lake Ladoga on the Finnish border. The Jesus Prayer was introduced by Abbot Nazarius, restorer of the monastery and former monk of Sarov (1735-1809). The Jesus Prayer was the source of many controversies and much misunderstanding, stemming from the confusion of four spiritual "givens": (1) constant prayer, (2) the invocation of the name of Jesus, (3) the Jesus Prayer, also known as the "Prayer of the Heart," (4) the "method" or ascetical technique which coordinated breathing with this prayer.

Saint Paul, in First Thessalonians (5:17) urges us to continual prayer. "Pray without ceasing." This unceasing prayer was not limited to one formula, but included petition, thanks, and praise.

The invocation of the name of God also goes back to the Bible. Saints Theodosius and Sergius recommended chanting the Psalms during work and between the services. While Saint Seraphim recommended the Jesus Prayer, he also suggested several other formulas of prayer and spoke of the invocation of the name of God. At the beginning of the twentieth century, this invocation was at the root of a spiritual movement among certain Russian monks of Athos, wrongly known as "deifiers of the name." They

151

called themselves "glorifiers of the name." The Holy Synod of Russia reacted swiftly against this movement, and the Athonite monks who belonged to it were returned to Russia by force.

The Jesus Prayer, as it was practiced at the monastery of Mount Sinai and later on Mount Athos ("Lord Jesus Christ, son of God, have mercy on me"), was not introduced in Russia until the time of Saint Nilus Sorsky and had a rather limited diffusion. The hesychast "method" was classed as a heresy in the Great Clerical Manual, published in 1913 by the Monastery of the Caves in Kiev. The manual stated that "the futile hesychast doctrine on the conditions for the reception of the uncreated divine light falls by itself into oblivion."

Russian spirituality is extremely varied and should be

A panorama of the monastery.

treated in several volumes, each one centered around a spiritual master. But it is Saint Sergius who is nevertheless the central figure, who demonstrates a middle way, without exaggerations and without concessions, completely faithful to the Gospel.

SAINT SERGIUS AND THE RUSSIAN PEOPLE

Saint Sergius and his monastery have always played a decisive role in the most difficult moments in the life of the Russian people. For five and a half centuries believers looked to the monastery of the Trinity. Thousands of pilgrims from all classes came to pray at the tomb of the one who had best incarnated the ideal of holiness. The Russian people are again today looking to Saint Sergius, and after forty years of trials, his monastery has again become the most important center of the religious life of Russia.

TRINITY LAVRA: A RELIGIOUS CENTER

During the fifteenth century, the Trinity Lavra grew under three remarkable abbots: Martinian (1447-55), Vassian (1455-66), who later became Archbishop of Rostov, and Paissy (1479-82), who intervened during the controversy over the monasteries' possessions. He was the only one of the abbots to speak out against the growing wealth of the monastery and especially against the necessity for the monks to manage lands where they did no work and where the peasants lived. Two successive abbots belonged to two opposing movements, but they never reached the extremes of the struggle between Joseph and Nilus Sorsky. Abbot Vassian, himself a former monk of the monastery of Saint Paphnutius, was one of Joseph's spiritual masters, and Abbot Paissy, who belonged to the monastic school of Saint Cyril of the White Lake, was one of Nilus Sorsky's spiritual guides. Saint Sergius' monastery maintained a conciliatory position between the two opposing camps during the second half of the century.

During the sixteenth century the monastery gave three metropolitans to the Russian Church: Simon, Joasaph and Cyril III, and its disciples played a great role in the foundation of new monasteries in the north. At the same time it became a monastery-fortress and one of the richest landowners in Russia. In 1540-1550 the monastery was surrounded by a stone enclosure topped by twelve towers. The surrounding villages formed a single large, active and commercial town. The solitude which the saint had so desired gave way to intense activity. The monastery owned nearly one hundred villages which had been given to it by princes and landowners, to which they added thirty more which they bought themselves. It also owned large fisheries and salt mines. The economos had to manage a fortune which surpassed that of many of the principalities. The revenues

154

The Trinity-Saint Sergius Monastery (17th c.)

155

were used for feeding pilgrims, who became more and more numerous, and for various charitable works. The monastery also added new churches. A chapel dedicated to Saint Sergius was built above the large entry porch. Another, dedicated to Saint Nikon, was built over his tomb at the time of his canonization in 1547. Ivan the Terrible had a particular veneration for Saint Sergius. He had a chapel dedicated to the holy abbot. The icon representing the appearance of the Virgin to Saint Sergius always accompanied the Russian armies. After the end of the wars against the Tartars and the victory over the Moslem kingdoms of Kazan and Astrakhan, the tsar established monasteries of Saint Sergius in these cities and began building a very large and beautiful church at the Trinity Lavra, dedicated to the Dormition of the Mother of God. This church, which was dedicated in 1585, still stands. It was returned to the Church in 1946.[17]

After the victory of Joseph Volokolamsk's disciples over the hermit monks from beyond the Volga and the trial of Maximus the Greek, the monastery of Saint Sergius spoke out in favor of those who were persecuted and Arthemius, the abbot, gave asylum to Maximus, who died peacefully in the monastery in 1556 and was buried there. However Abbot Arthemius was obliged to leave Russia five years later and continued his work at Sloutzk in Lithuania. In 1561, the Russian Church designated the Trinity-Saint Sergius Lavra as the first among all the monasteries of Russia. From then on it was the undisputed center of Russian religious life.

THE TRINITY LAVRA: A NATIONAL CENTER

From the beginning of the seventeenth century, the Trinity Lavra was also a rallying point for all the national forces. During the "time of troubles," it guided the people towards salvation, encouraged the weak, and worked for the restoration of the state after a terrible period of anarchy and destruction. Russia had known many bad years of invasion and destruction and civil wars, but two periods were particularly devastating: the great Mongol invasion of

1238-40 and the "time of troubles," 1605-13. In both cases it was largely due to Saint Sergius that moral and national direction was made possible. The dynasty of Rurik, which had reigned over Russia for seven centuries, vanished in 1598 with Ivan the Terrible's son Theodore. Boris Godunov, the brother of the last tsarina, was elected tsar of all Russia. He was a great diplomat and administrator who tried his best to improve the desperate situation in which Ivan the Terrible had left the country. Ivan's totalitarian and inhuman system had not only ruined the boyar class against which he was fighting but also the peasantry. The entire center of the country was devastated and totally depopulated. Several years of famine increased dissatisfaction, and when Boris Godunov died in 1605, the country almost immediately fell into anarchy. The new tsar, Basil Shuisky, had little authority and was threatened by imposters. The Polish and then the Swedish invaded the country. It was at this moment that the Lavra of Saint Sergius saved the country. The Polish army of Sapieha which marched on Moscow laid siege to the monastery, which was sheltering not only the populace of the surrounding areas, but also the

The siege of the monastery in 1608.

defenders of the Russian state. On September 23, 1608, the monastery was completely surrounded and the siege, which was to last sixteen months, began.

Simon Azariin, a chronicler of the mid-seventeenth century, wrote, "When the Muscovite state was ruined, when the cities, villages, and churches were destroyed by fire and sword, and when the country could find help nowhere, the Trinity-Saint Sergius Lavra flourished and lacked nothing, by the prayers of the all-holy Mother of God." The first general attack took place on September 30, and the Polish bombarded the monastery with the aid of 63 cannons. Abbot Joasaph and his helpers organized the life of the besieged monastery, and, on account of their help, the defenders were able to resist the numerous attacks, which lasted six weeks. All the Polish efforts were in vain. The overpopulation in the fortress was such that the monks could barely feed everyone, care for the wounded and bury the dead. In spring an epidemic of scurvy broke out and reduced the number of defenders from 2000 to 200. The attacks began again in May, 1609, and lasted throughout the summer. The monastery was finally liberated by the young Prince Skopin-Shuisky at the end of the year. By 1610 the monastery had yet another role. The Polish had besieged and pillaged Moscow, and an enormous number of wounded and dying came to the only place in Russia where they could hope to find help.

The great historian of Russia, S. Soloviev, describes the role of the Trinity Monastery in these terms: "When Moscow was attacked and when the men of Sapieha had burnt and pillaged the surrounding areas, crowds of refugees fled towards the monastery of the Trinity. The sight of this crowd of wounded, crippled and sick was terrifying. Many came to confess, receive Communion, and die near the walls of the monastery. Others died on the way. The monastery and the surrounding villages were full of wounded and dead. Then Abbot Dionysius, who had replaced Abbot Joasaph in 1610, called the economos, Abraham (Palitzin), the treasurer, all the brothers, the servants and the peasants from the neighboring villages, and beseeched them to help those who sought aid from Saint Sergius. The monastery paid for the food and all that was necessary to buy, but the men worked for free. They built hundreds of wooden houses, asylums and hospitals. Monks from the monastery visited all the surrounding area and brought back the wounded and dead. The women of the villages served without respite, washed the clothes of the living and prepared shrouds for the dead." Thus the monastery's treasures enabled it to relieve the sick and wounded. Only the monastery had the possibility of doing this, and it responded to its duty.

After 1610, Russia no longer had legal power. Tsar Basil was dismissed and the Polish occupied the capital. Patriarch Hermogen was imprisoned. In the summer of 1611, the monastery set out to save the fatherland. Just as the holy founder had decided the fate of Russia by blessing Prince Dmitri in 1380, so two centuries later his monastery headed the liberation movement. There were ten copyists in the abbot's cell, among whom was Alexis Tikhanov, who was the leading stenographer of his time. They sent messages to all the cities of Russia, calling the people to free Moscow and restore order. These messages, reaching the farthest corners of Russia, rallied failing spirits. Vain quarrels were forgotten and people united for the great cause of the liberation. One of the messages from the monastery reached the city of Nizhni-Novgorod, where it made a very great impression. Kuzma Minin, a rich businessman and one of the city's most prominent citizens, began a national collection to organize an army of liberation. The chronicle said that Saint Sergius appeared to him in a dream and ordered him to head the movement. Minin amassed enormous sums, enlisted the aid of a known military leader, Prince Pozharsky, and at the end of 1612 the army freed Moscow and re-established order in the country. When there were difficulties between the army and the Cossack troops, Abbot Dionysius offered to distribute all the monastery's treasures, but the Cossacks did not want this and decided to offer their services to the national leaders. The newly elected Tsar Michael Romanov visited the monastery of the Trinity on his way to Moscow. He returned on a pilgrimage after his coronation. The monastery of Saint Sergius had saved Russia, and after a period when it was totally devoted to the public welfare, it could finally return to its normal life.

The monastery in 1745.

However, a new task was awaiting it. The "time of troubles" had overthrown the life of the country. The populace had deserted the cities and fled into the forest. Thieves were along all the roads. It would be necessary to rebuild morals and to work for the reform of church life.

THE TRINITY LAVRA: A CENTER OF RENEWAL

After 1616, Abbot Dionysius (Zobninovsky) assembled all those who wished to participate in this renewal. Most of the reformers were admirers of Maximus the Greek and followed his plan for reform. Two problems occupied those who worked at the monastery: the correction of liturgical books and moral and religious renewal. They advocated a fight against certain popular feasts, which were often accompanied by debauchery, and also against disorder in the churches. They foresaw the institution of the obligatory Sunday sermon, which had completely fallen into disuse.

The monastery installed a printing press and published the lives of Saints Sergius and Nikon (1646-47). They also took measures to protect iconography against Western influences. Simon Azariin, a learned monk and chronicler, wrote *The Account of the Recent Miracles of Saint Sergius* and a book on the role of the monastery. Finally, in 1649 and 1654, one of the monks, Arsenius Sukhanov, made tours to Greece, Mount Athos and Palestine, and brought back more than 500 ancient manuscripts, which helped in correcting the liturgical books.

In the middle of the century, the "royal road" which led from Moscow to the monastery was clearly established. Until the construction of a railroad in 1862, it was the route of pilgrimage, marked with palaces where rulers stopped on their way to Saint Sergius. His importance could only be compared to that of Saint James of Compostella in the Middle Ages. Even Peter the Great and Catherine II, despite their fight against the monasteries, were faithful to him. The "royal road" (*Tsarsky Put*) left Moscow by the gate of the Cross, crossed the Wood of Mary and passed alongside a cemetery where the governor of Moscow, Count Rostopchin, was buried.

The tsars and empresses stopped there in large tents across from the Wood of Mary. It was there that Tsar Alexis stopped when taking his son, Peter the Great, then three years old, in 1675. The village, as well as the wood, belonged to the crown. There a palace later was built, where kings were received by authorities at the time of their return from the monastery. This palace was destroyed in 1812 and was never rebuilt. The village of Rostokin, not far from there, already belonged to the Trinity-Saint Sergius Lavra. It was confiscated by the state in 1764.

The road extended along the Yausa River and passed through Leonovo and Medvedkovo, which belonged to Prince Pozharsky. This latter village had an old church dating from the sixteenth century. The first palace where the tsars and empresses spent the night was built near the village of Tainitskoye. Tsar Alexis built a church there dedicated to the Annunciation, which Empress Elizabeth beautified. These were the two rulers who most often made pilgrimages to Saint Sergius' tomb.

The "royal road" continued towards the Great Mytischy, and on to Pushkino with its palaces for tsars and patriarchs. In the seventeenth and eighteenth centuries, the pilgrimages were carried out with great pomp. All of the people came out to see the tsar and gave him their petitions, as well as the traditional bread and salt. The tsar in turn would give alms to the poor.

The road continued past the Church of Saint Nicholas, built in 1642, and arrived at Bratovshchino, a village where there was a little palace in a thicket of birches. The tsars stopped there when they made pilgrimages on foot. The village church, dedicated to the Protection of the Holy Virgin, was built by Empress Anne. Empress Elizabeth, who particularly loved this place, built a second palace and arranged it for long stays. Nothing is left now of these buildings. The newly elected Tsar Michael was received by the clergy and boyars in Bratovshchino in 1613 before his solemn entrance into Moscow. In the village of Talitsy, pilgrims visited the caves dug out by the monk Anthony and continued their way towards the Khotkov monastery, where Saint Sergius' parents were buried. The monastery was rebuilt by Tsar Michael. Peter the Great did not dare to close it, but because he was hostile to the contemplative life of the nuns, he hired lacemakers from Bruges. They taught the art of Flemish lacemaking to the nuns, and this was carried on in the convent until the Revolution.

Beyond the monastery, the "royal road" reached the village Vozdvizhenskoye. There was a palace there, but the foundations, which later served for building a parish church, are all that remain. Three miles from there, on the high ground surrounded by the Pakhra River, was Radonezh, or rather what was left of this famous city, which had been destroyed by the Tartars. There was a wooden church, which was rebuilt in stone in the nineteenth century. The village around it was simply known as Gorodok ("little city"). Not far from there, on another plateau, a chapel and a large cross were erected where Saint Stephen of Perm greeted Saint Sergius on his way to Moscow. This was the last step before arriving at the monastery. The tsars and empresses descended from their carriages, prayed before the cross and often went the rest of the way on foot, passing the village Vokusha, where Abbot Dionysius had blessed the army of liberation in 1612. At the end of the seventeenth century, the Trinity-Saint Sergius Lavra twice played an

The monastery in the nineteenth century.

historical role. In 1682, the young tsars Peter and John took refuge there during a riot in 1689. Peter the Great fled there for a second time and stayed two months. All who supported the tsar came to the monastery, which for the moment became the provisional capital of the state.

Peter the Great, who believed that all the citizens of his empire should work for the state and who considered monasteries as centers of opposition to his reforms, began from the start of his reign a bitter struggle against the monks. He called them lazy, and termed the monasteries "the gangrene of the State." Monks were forbidden the use of paper and ink, and in 1723 Peter promulgated a law according to which no new monks could be received. However, he spared the Trinity Monastery out of respect for Saint Sergius and in thanksgiving for the protection which the monks had given him.

Empress Anne was the first to interfere with the life of the monastery. The abbot's power was replaced by a college of twelve old monks chosen by the Holy Synod. The government gave the monastery the title of "Lavra," which until that time had only been given to the Monastery of the

163

Caves in Kiev. Empress Elizabeth, who particularly venerated Saint Sergius and who often came to the monastery, had an 82-meter bell tower built. The plans were prepared by the famous Italian architect, Count Rastrelli, but the work was actually done by Russian architects in 1767. Catherine the Great did not dare to confiscate the monastery's goods at the time of the secularization of monasteries and only took away its lands. At that time there were 106,000 peasants working on the monastery's properties.

In 1742, a school was opened within the enclosures of the monastery, and in 1782, Metropolitan Platon founded the monastery of Bethany, not far from the Trinity-Saint Sergius Lavra. The lavra's library, which in the seventeenth century possessed more than 700 ancient manuscripts, grew even larger during the eighteenth century.

THE TRINITY LAVRA: A THEOLOGICAL CENTER

During the nineteenth century, the Trinity-Saint Sergius Monastery was the center of theological studies. In 1814, the Theological Academy had been transferred there from Moscow. There was also a seminary there. Of the three theological academies which existed in Russia, the one in Saint Petersburg was the most "worldly." It prepared its students for prominent positions in the Church, and life in the capital left its imprint on its former students. The school in Kiev, an heir of the academy founded at the beginning of the seventeenth century by Peter Moghila, followed the model of Roman Catholic universities. The academy in Moscow, situated far from the city, under the protection of Saint Sergius in the enclosure of his monastery, preserved Orthodox theology against secular models.

From 1770, the metropolitans of Moscow were abbots of the monastery. Metropolitan Philaret, theologian and eminent speaker, ruled for forty years (1821-67). The Theological Academy of Saint Sergius had the greatest specialists in theology, history and philosophy. Among them were the Rector Gorsky, and the professors Kliuchevsky and the two Golubinskys. At the end of the century, under the leadership of Archimandrite Anthony Khrapovitsky, the

The churches of the Trinity-Saint Sergius Monastery.

academy underwent a period of monastic renewal. In 1892, all of Russia celebrated the five hundredth anniversary of Saint Sergius' death. At that time, the lavra held thirteen churches within its walls, dedicated to the Trinity (with the tomb of Saint Sergius), the Dormition (pro-cathedral), Saint Nikon, the Descent of the Holy Spirit (with the tomb of Maximus the Greek), Saint Sergius, the Nativity, Saint John the Baptist, the Vision of the Virgin, Our Lady,

165

Saints Zosima and Sabbatius, the Martyrs Anastasia and
Barbara, and Saints Peter and Paul, as well as two chapels.
Because of the number of pilgrims, one million a year,
the services were celebrated during the summer every day
in the thirteen churches.

The monastery's museum holds an enormous number
of chalices, gold Gospel books, precious clothes, crosses and
miters, and more than 7000 books (not counting those of
the rich library of the Theological Academy). The monastery also had a school of iconography with sixty students
who received a free education. There was also a painting
studio in which forty specialists worked. A school for singing dealt especially with the harmonization of ancient mel-
odies. There was an asylum for 180 incurables, a hospital,

a school for orphans and, outside of the walls, an asylum and a hospital for women and a school for 250 boys from the neighboring villages.

The last tsar of Russia, Nicholas II, who was very pious, often came to the lavra. It was still a center for crowds of pilgrims and many intellectuals until the Revolution in 1917. In October 1917, Patriarch Tikhon went to the lavra for prayer and meditation after his election.

In 1922, it was plundered during the confiscation of church goods. It was closed for worship and became the center of Communist studies and anti-religious propaganda. The remainder of its artistic riches were taken to the museum of the town of Saint Sergius, which was renamed Zagorsk ("beyond the mountains"). On Easter 1946, the monastery was reopened for worship and the restoration of the religious buildings began. The Theological Academy opened again in 1948. By 1950, the large popular pilgrimages had begun again. That of July 5, 1950, the feast day of Saint Sergius, was one of the most impressive. The service was celebrated in three restored churches by Patriarch Alexis and numerous clergy.

At the Trinity-Saint Sergius Monastery, it is possible to buy crosses and icons and many people go there to purchase them. Thus, despite the forty years of the Communist regime, Saint Sergius continues to be a spiritual guide of the Russian people, and his monastery has become once again the center for all those who thirst for truth and justice.

Portable Icon (16th c.), Trinity-St. Sergius Museum.

SAINT SERGIUS AND THE WEST

Between 1920 and 1925, more than a million Russians left their country and were spread throughout the entire world. They frequently centered around churches which they built. They needed clergy to serve their newly created parishes. The question was particularly acute in Paris, which was the cultural center of the emigration. The Rue Daru church alone was no longer enough, for the numbers of Orthodox had increased tenfold in just a few years. They dreamed of building a second church which would be a monastery and a theological school. Since all of the monasteries and theological schools had been closed in Russia, it was necessary to carry on the Russian monastic and theological tradition where this could be done freely.

An unexpected opportunity arose for the Russian émigrés. The French government was auctioning some German Protestant property which had been put under sequester at the beginning of the war. The bid by far surpassed the means of the Russian colony, but Metropolitan Evlogy, head of the Russian Church in Western Europe, supported by M. M. Ossorguine, initiator of this purchase, decided to enter the auction, and the necessary sum was collected in time. All of the emigration took an active part in this collection. Protestant friends also contributed to the purchase of the property, which took place on July 5, 1924, the feast of Saint Sergius. The church was consecrated in February, 1925, and the theological school opened its doors in May of the same year. The Church of Saint Sergius was painted in the style of the old Russian churches by the famous iconographer, D. Stelletsky. While being the second Russian parish in Paris, the church on the Rue de Crimée was from its beginning a "Podvorye" (an affiliate of a monastery), and its superiors were always monks: Archimandrite John (later bishop) and Archimandrite Sergius. Thus the continuation of the uninterrupted monastic tradition in Russia was carried out. Saint Sergius also housed a free dispensary for sick Russians and a candle factory. Next to the

Iconostasis of the Church of Saint Sergius in Paris.

monastic church was the Institute of Orthodox Theology, which soon became an important center of study. It was a school for preparing priests for the diaspora parishes and a place for meeting with the different Christian denominations.

Metropolitan Evlogy, who was rector of the Institute for twenty years, studied at the Saint Sergius Theological Academy in the Trinity Lavra. Two of the professors, Fr. Sergius Bulgakov and Sergius Besobrasov (later Bishop Cassian), bore the name of the holy founder of the monastery. The parish and the Institute were both placed under the protection of Saint Sergius and became known as the Saint Sergius Institute.

Archimandrite Kiprian organized liturgical weeks which involved non-Orthodox. Exchanges of professors took place soon, and the teaching body took an active part in all ecumenical conferences and meetings. Many famous personalities belonging to different Christian denominations visited Saint Sergius'. On January 30 of each year, Christians of all denominations especially gathered at Saint Sergius' for the Feast of the Three Hierarchs (Saints Basil,

172

Gregory Nazianzen and John Chrysostom), at which the Liturgy was served in Greek and was followed by a fraternal meal.

The Institute has a good library and an office of Christian education and publishes a magazine (*Orthodox Thought*). The professors at the Institute have published several hundreds of books and articles. The bibliography of their works makes up a fascicle of 100 pages. The Institute's choir has toured the countries of Europe, bringing the riches of ancient liturgical chant to the Western world. Alumni of the Institute are spread throughout the world and have kept the school's traditions. It is interesting to note that an American friend of the Institute, D. A. Lowrie, has written a history of the Institute, entitled *Saint Sergius in Paris.*

The school was also the source of the Brotherhood of Saint Sergius, which brought together students and alumni of the Institute. They published a series of "St. Sergius pamphlets" which continued the series of popular editions printed by the Trinity Lavra. They also published liturgical texts with commentaries.

Another center of contact between Eastern and Western Christians, which has its seat in London, also took Saint Sergius as one of its patrons. It is the Fellowship of Saint Alban and Saint Sergius. It was founded in 1928 in order to create closer relations between Anglicans and Orthodox, but it accepts Protestant and Catholic members. It organizes annual conferences in England, in which participate not only professionals but also students, so that the younger generation can work to understand and know each other better. In 1935, it established a center in London, known as Saint Basil's House (52 Ladbroke Grove). It has a chapel, a library, an English magazine entitled *Sobornost*, and has published several books on Orthodoxy, including one by N. Zernov on Saint Sergius. Thus the two centers for rapprochement between Western and Eastern Christians in Europe both have as their patron Saint Sergius, who, six centuries after his death, continues to give the example of a life entirely conformed to the Gospel ideal and which continually renews itself according to the needs of the life of the Church.

173

Chronology

	EAST	WEST
860-865	Mission to the Slavs by Saints Cyril and Methodius	Disintegration of Charlemagne's Empire
936-973		Otto I
954-955	Baptism of Saint Olga	Norman invasions of France
959-960	Delegation from Olga to Otto I and mission of Adalbert of Trier to Kiev	
964-1015	Saint Vladimir	
987		Hugh Capet
988	Baptism of Saint Vladimir and the Kievans	
993-1073	Saint Anthony of Kiev	
1019-1054	Yaroslav the Wise, Grand Prince of Kiev	
1025	Construction of the Saint Sophia Cathedral in Kiev	
1040-1450	Establishment of the Monastery of the Caves in Kiev	
1045	Construction of the Saint Sophia Cathedral in Novgorod	
1051		Anna of Kiev (daughter of Yaroslav), Queen of France and wife of Henry I, crowned at Reims
1054	Disintegration of the Kievan Empire	Schism between Rome and Byzantium
1056		Norman conquest of England
1075-1122		Conflict between the Papacy and the Empire
1096-1191		The first three crusades
1091-1153		Bernard of Clairvaux
1150-1220	Saint Abraham of Smolensk	
1182-1226		Francis of Assisi

1204		Constantinople taken and sacked by the Crusaders
1208-1278		Crusade against the Albigensians
1215-1270		Saint Louis, King of France
1216-1236	Saint Alexander Nevsky	
1238-1240	Mongol invasion; destruction of Kiev	
1298-1378	Saint Alexis, Metropolitan of Moscow	
1305-1377		Popes at Avignon
1314-1392	Saint Sergius	
1325	Moscow becomes religious center of Russia	
1337-1453		The Hundred Years War
1340-1396	Saint Stephen of Perm	
1346		Battle of Crecy
1356		Battle of Poitiers
1360-1430	Andrew Rublev	
1371	Shearers' heresy in Novgorod	
1378-1417		Great Western Schism
1380	Battle of Kulikovo	
1384		Death of John Wyclif
1409	Construction of the Church of the Holy Trinity	
1387-1455		Fra Angelico
1417		Council of Constance
1422	Canonization of Saint Sergius	
1431		Council of Basel; death of Joan of Arc
1433-1508	Saint Nilus Sorsky	
1439-1515	Saint Joseph of Volokolamsk	Council of Florence
1448	Russian Church gains autocephaly	
1453	Fall of Constantinople	
1461	Rise of the theory of "Moscow, the Third Rome"	
1471	The Judaizers	
1475-1479	Cathedral of the Dormition in Moscow, built by the Italian architect, Fioravanti	

176

The bell tower.

Saint Sergius

1314   May 3: Bartholomew is born in Rostov the Great

1321   Bartholomew is sent to school

1328   Bartholomew flees Rostov with his family and goes to Radonezh

1334   Death of his parents; departure for the wilderness

1337   October 7: He becomes a monk and receives the name Sergius

1340   Establishment of the Holy Trinity Monastery

1344   Sergius is ordained priest and becomes abbot

1347   Arrival of Archimandrite Simon; larger church is built

1350   Stephen, Sergius' elder brother, and his son, John (Theodore), return to the Trinity Lavra

1350-1355 First miracles

1355   Introduction of the cenobitic life

1358   Establishment of the Monastery of the Savior in Moscow

1358   First peace-mission to Rostov

1358   Sergius leaves the Lavra and goes to live on the banks of the Kirzhach

1362   Sergius returns to his monastery

1363   Second peace-mission to Rostov

1365   Mission to Nizhni-Novgorod

1370   Establishment of the Monastery of the Holy Virgin in Moscow

1374   Establishment of the Monastery of the Holy Virgin in Serpukhov

1378   Metropolitan Alexis proposes that Sergius succeed him

1380   September 8: Battle of Kulikovo

1385   Establishment of the Monastery of the Theophany in Kolomna

1385   Peace mission to Riazan

1392   September 25: Sergius dies

1408   The Trinity Lavra is destroyed by the Tartars

1409-1411 The Lavra is rebuilt by Nikon

1422   July 5: Discovery of the relics and canonization of Saint Sergius

St. Sergius, embroidery (ca. 1422).

Notes

[1]The canonization of saints in the Orthodox Church is at the initiative of the local autocephalous (self-governing) church. The Russian Church became autocephalous only in 1448. Hence the difficulties in the canonization of Saints Boris and Gleb.

[2]Their proper names are: "The Lavra of the Caves" in Kiev and "The Trinity Lavra." A lavra is a large monastery having several churches within its enclosure. Before 1917, there were four lavras in Russia: Kiev, Trinity-Saint Sergius, Saint Alexander Nevsky in Petrograd and Pochaev in Volynia. Their abbot was the bishop of the diocese and they were governed by a vicar-abbot, assisted by a council. On Mount Athos there was only one lavra, that of Saint Athanasius, the "Great Lavra."

[3]The years are sometimes indicated by double dates because Russia used the Roman calendar (with the year beginning on March 1) until 1343, and from 1343 to 1699, the ecclesiastical calendar which starts on September 4. In the ancient chronicles, events are dated from the Creation of the World (5525 before our era) which often makes a precise calculation rather difficult.

[4]This was actually a room set aside for prayers. Peasants kept their icons in a corner of the main room, known as the "beautiful corner." The Old Believers still kept the practice of a room for family prayers up until the Revolution.

[5]The Orthodox Church celebrates the feast of the Holy Apostles Barnabas and Bartholomew on June 11. August 25 is the feast of the translation of Saint Bartholomew's relics.

[6]The word *kremlin* is not restricted to Moscow. Originally, all fortresses were known as *kremlins*, but after the construction of the *kremlin* in Moscow, at the end of the fifteenth century, the word gradually became a proper noun, henceforth referring to the fortress in Moscow.

[7]The Orthodox Church uses leavened bread for the Liturgy. A piece of bread which will serve for communion is removed. The rest of this bread is given to the faithful at the end of the Liturgy. During the preparation, pieces are taken out in memory of the Mother of God, the saints, the living and the dead and placed around the Lamb on the paten. At the end of the Liturgy, the priest or the deacon puts them into the chalice, saying: "Wash away, O Lord, the sins of all those remembered here, by Thy precious Blood; through the prayers of Thy Saints."

[8]The term "dormition" is an exact translation of the Slavonic word *uspenie* (*koimesis* in Greek). The cathedrals of the Holy Wisdom were dedicated to the Christ, the Divine Wisdom, in Greece and to the Theotokos in Russia. The cathedral in Kiev celebrated its patronal feast on September 8,

the feast of the Nativity of the Theotokos, and the one in Novgorod celebrated on August 15, the feast of the Dormition.

[9]The "Golden Horde" was a state founded by the Tartars in 1242 on the lower Volga. Its capital was Sarai. Russian princes and bishops had to go there to receive the *yarlyk*, which confirmed their rights and the rights of the Church. The Golden Horde was divided into two kingdoms, that of Kazan and that of Astrakhan. They were both taken over by Ivan the Terrible in the middle of the sixteenth century.

[10]In Russia, distances were calculated in *versts*. One *verst* equals 1,060 meters. Rostov the Great is 222 kilometers from Moscow, Radonezh 60 kilometers, and the lavra is 70 kilometers from Radonezh. The monastery of Khotkovo is half-way between the lavra and Radonezh. It is impossible to find Radonezh on a map. It was destroyed by the Polish in 1610 and was never rebuilt. The village which is closest to its location new bears the name Gorodok ("little city"). The village around the lavra is now called Zagorsk ("the city beyond the mountains"). All of the other locales mentioned in this book have retained their original names.

[11]The Orthodox Church calls monastic saints "righteous." This term is rarely used in the West; it can be rendered simply as "blessed" or "saint."

[12]The Russian Church was under the Patriarch of Constantinople, who appointed the metropolitans. They were either Russian or Greek. If they were Russian they had to go to Constantinople to receive their "investiture" from the Patriarch. The Russian Church did not become autocephalous (self-governing) until 1448.

[13]The title of archimandrite is usually translated as abbot and that of hegumen as prior. Abbots were the heads of large monasteries, while heads of less important monasteries were known as priors. The distinction between abbey and priory does not exist in the East. On Mount Athos, only the large monasteries are known as "abbeys" while the others are called sketes. The title of archimandrite is now bestowed "honorarily." Priest-monks who are neither archimandrites nor hegumens are known as hieromonks. Monastic deacons are called hierodeacons.

[14]The canonarch is the singer who announces the verses, which are repeated after him by the choir.

[15]The iconostasis is a partition which separates the sanctuary from the rest of the church. It was originally rather low but it now is five "stories" in some churches. The iconostasis has three doors. The Royal Doors, those in the center, may be entered only by priests and deacons. The Royal Doors open directly onto the altar table, which is in the middle of the sanctuary. They symbolize the Gospel, which leads towards the throne of God. The Annunciation, which is the beginning of our salvation, and the four evangelists are depicted on the Royal Doors.

The northern and southern doors bear icons of archangels and martyrs. Processions usually pass through the northern door.

To the right of the Royal Doors there is always an icon of Christ as teacher and to the left, an icon of the Mother of God with the child Christ. Further on the iconostasis there are the icons of the patron saint of the church and the patron saint of the country. Above the Royal Doors there is usually the icon of the Last Supper and on the second "story," the twelve great feasts of the liturgical year.

[16]The Church of the Protection of the Holy Virgin was built in 1556 at the order of Ivan the Terrible by the Russian architects, Postnik and Barma, to commemorate the victory over the Tartars. It is on the great Square of

Moscow, which is incorrectly called "Red Square." *Krasnaia Ploshchad'* really means the Beautiful Square. The Church of the Protection, which is commonly known as the Church of Saint Basil the Blessed (*Khram Vasilia Blazhennogo*), is now a museum.

[17]The author has used the term cathedral only to translate the Russian words: *Kafedral'nyi sobor*. The erroneous translation of the word *sobor* as cathedral is so fixed in the West that one often hears the ridiculous statement, "the cathedrals of the Kremlin." Moscow was an exception in having two cathedrals before the Revolution: the Temple of Christ the Savior (*Khram Khrista Spasitelia*), which was the cathedral of the city and of the diocese of Moscow; and the Cathedral of the Dormition in the Kremlin, which was the cathedral of the entire Russian Church. *Sobor* should be translated as "the main church." *Sobors* had a larger staff of clergy than did the parish churches. There was a *sobor* in the main part of every area, in the large abbeys and several in the large cities.

Iconographic Sources

There are several icons of Saint Sergius which date from the beginning of the fifteenth century and are contemporary to his canonization. An embroidered cloth of Saint Sergius (1422) which covered his shrine is kept in the Zagorsk Museum. Among the illustrated manuscripts, it is important to note that of the library of the Academy of Sciences (no. 34-3-4), which dates from the fifteenth century, and that of Moscow (no. 8663), which dates from the sixteenth century. The latter is the more important and contains more than 300 color miniatures. Some of the miniatures from these manuscripts were published in Archimandrite Nikon's edition of the "Life" as well as in other publications. However, this is the first time that a microfilm was made of all of the miniatures in manuscript no. 8663, a selection of which was used to illustrate this book.

A series of pictures on the life of Saint Sergius was painted by M. Nesterov at the end of the nineteenth and beginning of the twentieth centuries. The inventory of the miniatures, icons and religious items kept in the Trinity-Saint Sergius Lavra was published after the Revolution by Yuri Olsufiev (Zagorsk, 1920, 1921 and 1926).

Hagiographic Sources

The Life of Saint Sergius, written by his disciple Epiphanius the Wise around 1417-1418; published by Archimandrite Leonid in *Monuments of*

Ancient Literature, vol. LVIII, St. Petersburg, 1885. A bibliography of the other editions of the *Life* can be found in E. Golubinsky's book: *Saint Sergius of Radonezh and the Lavra of the Trinity Which He Founded*, Zagorsk, 1892.

The Life of Saint Sergius, by Pachomius the Logothete, published in the *Menologion* of Metropolitan Macarius, vol. III, September, St. Petersburg, 1883. This volume also contains the *Life* written by Epiphanius.

The Great Lives of Saints, collected by Metropolitan Macarius of Moscow, from 1532 to 1552, 27,000 pages in-folio. The months of September, October and April are published in full. November, December and January are partial; by the Commission of Archaeography, St. Petersburg, 1868-1917.

Complete Collection of Russian Chronicles. The most valuable chronicle, which contained the episcopal annals of Rostov and the annals of the Trinity-Saint Sergius Lavra, perished during the burning of Moscow in 1812.

Life of Saint Stephen of Perm, by Epiphanius the Wise, published by Kuchelev-Bezborodko, in *Monuments of Ancient Russian Literature*, vol. IV, St. Petersburg, 1862.

The Life of Saint Alexis, Metropolitan of Moscow, by Pachomius the Logothete, published by Chliakov, in Reports of the Second Section of the Academy of Sciences, St. Petersburg, 1914.

The Life of Saint Nikon of Radonezh, by Pachomius the Logothete, published by Yablonsky as an appendix to his book *Pachomius the Serbian*, St. Petersburg, 1908.

Excerpts from the *Life of Saint Sergius* are also published in Russian translation in "Saint Sergius Pamphlets," No. 12, Paris, 1928.

Select Bibliography

Works in Russian devoted to Saint Sergius and his times:

Artskhovsky, A. V., *Ancient Russian Miniatures as Historical Sources*, Moscow, 1944.

Bulgakov, S., "The Spiritual Heritage of Saint Sergius," *Put'* no. 5, Y.M.C.A. Press, Paris, 1926.

Bulgakov, S., *Great Manual for Clergy*, Lavra of the Caves, Kiev, 1913.

Chamurin, G., *Rostov the Great and the Lavra of Saint Sergius* (*Treasures of Russian Art*, vol. VI), Moscow, 1913.

Eding, B. von, *Rostov the Great* (in the series *Russian Cities, Centers of Art*, ed. I. Grabar), Moscow, 1913.

Eingorn, V., *The Significance for Russian History of Saint Sergius and of the Monastery which He Founded*, Moscow, 1889.

Florensky, P., *The Trinity-Saint Sergius Lavra and Russia*, Moscow, 1919.

Fedotov, G., *The Saints of Ancient Russia*, Y.M.C.A. Press, Paris, 1931.

Golubinsky, E., *Saint Sergius of Radonezh and the Lavra which He Founded*, Zagorsk, 1892.

Gorsky, A. V., *Historical Description of the Lavra of Saint Sergius*, Moscow, 1890.

Guide to the Trinity-Saint Sergius Lavra, third edition, Moscow, 1886.

Kazansky, P., *History of Russian Orthodox Monasticism*, Moscow, 1855.

Kadloubovsky, A., *An Essay on the History of the Ancient Lives of the Saints*, Warsaw, 1902.

Kliuchevsky, B., *Saint Sergius, Spiritual Teacher of the Russian People* (*Essays and Lectures*, vol. III, Moscow, 1913).

_____, *The Ancient Lives of Saints as Historical Sources*, Moscow, 1871.

Kudriavtsev, F. F., *History of Monasticism in North-East Russia after Saint Sergius*, Moscow, 1881.

Nikon, Archimandrite, *An Illustrated Life of Saint Sergius*, Zagorsk, 1898.

Okhotin, J., *A Description of the Monastery of Saint Abraham of Rostov*, Yaroslavl, 1862.

Pushkarev, S., *The Trinity-Saint Sergius Lavra*, Prague, no date.

Roerich, C. de, *The Banner of Saint Sergius*, Riga, 1934.

Rogovich, A., *The Lavra of Saint Sergius and Its Founder*, Grad Kitezh Press, Berlin, 1922.

Titov, A., *The Kremlin of Rostov*, Moscow, 1912.

Vinogradov, N., *The Lavra of Saint Sergius*, Moscow, 1944.

Zaitsev, B. K., *Saint Sergius of Radonezh*, Y.M.C.A. Press, Paris, 1925.

See also the standard histories of the Russian Church, by Bishop Macarius, Bishop Philaret and E. Golubinsky; and, for the more recent period, *The Messenger of the Moscow Patriarchate*, 1947.

Works in Western languages pertaining especially to Saint Sergius:

Hackel, Alexej A., *Sergij von Radonesh*, Verlag Regensburg, Münster, 1956.

Zaitsev, Boris, *Saint Serge de Radonège*, French trans. by I. Kovalevsky, "Le Roseau d'Or," no. 30 (6), Plon, Paris, 1928.

Zernov, Nicholas, *Saint Sergius, Builder of Russia*, S.P.C.K., London, 1945.

Books and articles pertaining to Russian spirituality and monasticism:

Arseniev, Nicholas, *Holy Moscow*, S.P.C.K., London, 1946.

_____, *Russian Piety*, The Faith Press, London, 1964.

_____, "Saints et Starets russes," in *Dieu Vivant*, vol. VI, Paris, 1947.

Behr-Sigel, Elizabeth, *Prière et Sainteté dans l'Église Russe*, Editions du Cerf, Paris, 1950.

Bouyer, Louis, "Les catholiques occidentaux et la liturgie byzantine," in *Dieu Vivant, vol.* XXI, Paris, 1952.

Florovsky, George, "Russian Missions: An Historical Sketch," *The Christian East*, vol. XIV, no. 1 (1933), pp. 30-41.

Hackel, Alexis, *Les icônes russes*, preface by Daniel-Rops, Editions de Chévetogne, Belgium, 1956.

Icône de la Sainte Trinité d'André Roublev, Editions de Chévetogne, Belgium, no date.

Kronstadt, John of, *My Life in Christ*, English trans., Jordanville, N. Y., no date.

Kologrivof, John, *Essai sur la sainteté en Russie*, Edition Beyaert, Bruges, 1953.

Kovalevsky, Pierre, *Manuel d'histoire russe*, Payot, Paris, 1948.

_____, "La chrétienté orientale orthodoxe et ses divers aspects nationaux," *Revue de Psychologie des Peuples*, Le Havre, 1953 (1).

Leib, Bernard, *Rome, Kiev et Byzance*, Vrin, Paris, 1924.

Lossky, Vladimir, *The Mystical Theology of the Eastern Church*, James Clark & Co., London, 1957.

Lot-Borodine, Myrra, *La doctrine de la liberté et de la grâce dans l'orthodoxie gréco-orientale*, Jacques et Demontrond, Besançon, 1938-39.

Meyendorff, Jean, "Partisans et ennemis des biens ecclésiastiques au sein du monachisme russe," *Irenikon*, vol. XXIX, no. 1 and 2 (1956).

Ouspensky, Leonid, and Vladimir Lossky, *The Meaning of Icons*, Boston Book and Art Shop, Boston, 1969.

Pascal, Pierre, "La religion du peuple russe," *Revue de Psychologie des Peuples*, Le Havre, 1947 (2 and 3).

_____, *Avvakum et les débuts du Rascol*, Mouton, Paris, 1963.

The Prayer of Jesus, by a monk of the Eastern Church, Desclée, New York, 1967.

Récits d'un pèlerin russe à son père spirituel, Editions La Baconnière, Neuchâtel, 1943.

Rouet de Journel, *Le monachisme russe et les monastères russes*, Payot, Paris, 1957.

Spiridon, Archimandrite, *Mes missions en Sibérie*, Editions du Cerf, Paris, 1950.

Schubart, Walter, *L'Europe et l'âme de l'Orient*, Albin Michel, Paris, 1949.

Tyszkiewicz, Stanislas, and Théodore Belpaire, *Ascètes russes*, Editions du Soleil Levant, Namur, 1957.

Zander, Valentine, *Saint Seraphim of Sarov*, St. Vladimir's Seminary Press, Crestwood, N. Y., 1975.

Saint Sergius and the West:

Lowrie, Donald, *Saint Sergius in Paris*, S.P.C.K., London, 1954.

Sobornost, a journal published by the Society of Saint Alban and Saint Sergius, London, 1935—.

The Illustrations

The following illustrations were microfilmed from the manuscript of the sixteenth century *Life of St. Sergius* in the Lenin Library in Moscow: pp. 31, 32, 52, 54, 61, 64, 65, 67, 68, 70, 73, 74, 75, 77, 79, 80, 82, 84, 87, 88, 90, 91, 93, 95, 96, 98, 99, 100, 102, 105, 108, 112, 115, 118, 120, 122, 124, 129, 134. *The History of Russian Art,* by Igor Grabar (Moscow, 1958), pp. 19, 24, 25, 41, 45, 46, 50, 131, 132, 136-37, 153. Boudot-Lamotte: pp. 27, 49, 125, 126, 165. Roger Viollet: p. 35. Speiser: pp. 160, 163, 178. Giraudon: p. 47, 145. Photographic archives: p. 150. Komatowitsch, *Die Urgestalt der Brüder Karamasoff:* p. 148.

Index

Philaret, Metropolitan of Kiev (Bishop of Kaluga): 149
Philaret, Metropolitan of Moscow: 164
Philotheus, Patriarch of Constantinople: 100
Phocas, Bardas: 21
Photius, Patriarch of Constantinople: 13, 15
Peter, brother of St. Sergius: 64, 66, 76
Peter (St.), Metropolitan of Moscow: 59-60, 73
Peter (St.), of Rostov: 63, 71
Peter the Great, Emperor of Russia: 144-146, 161-163
Peter Moghila, Metropolitan of Kiev: 164
Platon, Metropolitan of Moscow: 164
Pozharsky, Prince: 159, 161
Procopius (St.), of Ustiug: 42, 128

Rublev, Andrei: 106-107, 123

Sabbas (St.), of Dubensky monastery: 126-127
Sabbatius (St.), of Solovky: 138-139
Samuel, King of the Bulgars: 17
Sapieha of Poland: 157
Seraphim (St.), of Sarov: 119, 148, 151
Sergius (St.), of Nurom: 127
Simeon, King of the Bulgars: 16
Simon, Abbot: 89, 99
Simon, Ecclesiarch of the Trinity: 117
Simon, monk of the Trinity (chronicler): 157, 160
Stephen, brother of St. Sergius: 64, 66, 76-78, 90, 101-102, 107, 114
Stephen, Abbot of Makhrishchi: 103-104
Stephen (St.), Bishop of Perm: 60, 128-130, 162
Sviatopolk, Prince of Kiev: 28-30
Sviatoslav, Prince of Kiev: 17, 19
Sylvester (St.), of Obnosk: 127

Theodore I, Tsar of Russia: 156
Theodore (John), Archbishop of Rostov, nephew of St. Sergius: 75, 90, 107-108
Theodore, Prince of Rostov: 72
Theodosius (St.), of Kiev: 34-36, 39, 65, 91, 103, 142, 148, 151
Theognostus, Metropolitan of Moscow: 76-78, 85-86, 114
Theophanes (Govorov), Bishop of Vladimir: 151
Tikhon, Patriarch of Moscow: 167
Tikhon (St.), of Zadonsk: 147
Tokhtamysh, Tartar Khan: 113, 123
Tryphon (St.), of Pechenga: 139

Vassian, Abbot of the Trinity: 154
Vassilko, Prince of Rostov: 59, 71
Vladimir (St.), Prince of Kiev: 19-24, 28, 50
Vladimir Monomachos, Prince of Kiev: 37-38
Vladimir, Prince of Serpukhov: 109, 112, 116
Vsevolod, Prince of Novgorod: 38
Vsevolod, Prince of Rostov: 72

Yaroslav the Wise, Prince of Kiev: 24-26, 53
Yuri, Prince of Moscow: 56

Zossima, Abbot of Solovky: 138-139